Part 1
ABSOLUTE BEGINNER

Rex Jones II, CSTE, TMap

Java 4
Selenium
WebDriver

Come Learn
How To Program
For Automation
Testing

This book only covers
Java which is one of the
programming languages
for Selenium

Free Webinars, Videos, and Live Training

Mr. Jones plans to have **free** step-by-step demonstration webinars, videos, and live trainings walking people through concepts of Selenium and QTP/UFT from A - Z. The material will teach/train individuals the fundamentals of the programming language, fundamentals of Selenium and QTP/UFT, and important concepts of Selenium and QTP/UFT. All of the webinars, videos, and live training will be directed toward beginners as well as mid-level automation engineers.

Sign Up to Receive

1. 3 Tips To Master Selenium Within 30 Days
   http://tinyurl.com/3-Tips-For-Selenium

2. 3 Tips To Master QTP/UFT Within 30 Days
   http://tinyurl.com/3-Tips-For-QTP-UFT

3. Free Webinars, Videos, and Live Trainings
   http://tinyurl.com/Free-QTP-UFT-Selenium

Skype: rex.jones34
Twitter: @RexJonesII
Email: Rex.Jones@Test4Success.org
LinkedIn: https://www.linkedin.com/in/rexjones34

Rex Jones' Contact Information

Email Address: Rex.Jones@Test4Success.org
LinkedIn: https://www.linkedin.com/in/rexjones34
Books: http://tinyurl.com/Rex-Allen-Jones-Books
Twitter: @RexJonesII
Skype: rex.jones34

3 Tips To Master Selenium Within 30 Days
http://tinyurl.com/3-Tips-For-Selenium

Free Webinars, Videos, and Live Trainings
http://tinyurl.com/Free-QTP-UFT-Selenium

Table of Contents

Skype: rex.jones34
Twitter: @RexJonesII
Email: Rex.Jones@Test4Success.org
LinkedIn: https://www.linkedin.com/in/rexjones34

3 Tips To Master Selenium Within 30 Days
http://tinyurl.com/3-Tips-For-Selenium

Free Webinars, Videos, and Live Trainings
http://tinyurl.com/Free-QTP-UFT-Selenium

Skype: rex.jones34
Twitter: @RexJonesII
Email: Rex.Jones@Test4Success.org
LinkedIn: https://www.linkedin.com/in/rexjones34

Preface

I am enthused to write an instructional book on Java because I have talked with many testers who can relate to the frustration caused by the lack of information to learn Java for automation testing. Java is one of the programming languages for Selenium. A common challenge with new automation testers is learning how to program. Therefore, this book is designed to help an absolute beginner learn Java. The purpose of this book is to fill a need of automation testers who are forced to hurry past the programming component of automation, leading to a struggle with working in Selenium.

Target Audience

The target audience is beginners with little to no knowledge of Java. Beginners are people new to Selenium and Java, and have a desire to establish a deep foundation of Java principles.

Why learn Java?

Java is a powerful programming language that is frequently and commonly implemented in the Information Technology (IT) industry. Java programmers are in high demand in the IT field and being able to code automation scripts in Java will make you a commodity to any quality assurance testing team. There are many Java forums (message boards) online that support Java programmers in need of a solution for a problem. Learning Java and Selenium is a great combination that will make any quality assurance tester effective on an automation project.

About the Author

Rex Allen Jones II is a QA/Software Tester with a passion for sharing knowledge about testing software. He has been watching webinars, attending seminars, and testing applications over 10 years. Mr. Jones graduated from DeVry University with a Bachelor's of Science degree in Computer Information Systems (CIS).

Rex is an author, consultant, and former Board of Director for User Group: Dallas / Fort Worth Mercury User Group (DFWMUG) and member of User Group: Dallas / Fort Worth Quality Assurance Association (DFWQAA). In addition to his User Group memberships, he is a Certified Software Tester Engineer (CSTE) and has a Test Management Approach (TMap) certification.

Mr. Jones' advice for people interested in Automation Testing is to learn the programming language. This advice led him to write 4 programming books "(Part 1 & Part 2) You Must

Skype: rex.jones34
Twitter: @RexJonesII
Email: Rex.Jones@Test4Success.org
LinkedIn: https://www.linkedin.com/in/rexjones34

About the Author   (Part 1) Java 4 Selenium WebDriver

Learn VBScript for QTP/UFT" and "(Part 1 & Part 2) Java 4 Selenium WebDriver". VBScript is the programming language for Unified Functional Testing (UFT) formerly known as Quick Test Professional (QTP) and Java is one of the programming languages for Selenium WebDriver.

In addition to the 4 programming books, Mr. Jones wrote 2 more books. The 5th book is named Absolute Beginner (Part 1) Selenium WebDriver for Functional Automation Testing which provides a deep foundation of Selenium WebDriver. Finally, a 6th book named Getting Started With TestNG (A Java Test Framework). All books are available in Paperback, eBook, and PDF.

3 Tips To Master Selenium Within 30 Days
http://tinyurl.com/3-Tips-For-Selenium

Free Webinars, Videos, and Live Trainings
http://tinyurl.com/Free-QTP-UFT-Selenium

About the Editor

When Samantha Mann is not improving the contents of a document through constructive editing marks and remarks, she is enjoying life as a professional in Dallas, Texas. Samantha is a User Experience guru in the realms of research and design, and works as an Information Technology consultant. Outside of work her hobbies include the typical nerd-type fun of freelance editing, reading, writing, and binge watching Netflix with her pitbull.

Connect with Samantha:

Samantha.danae.mann@gmail.com

https://www.linkedin.com/pub/samantha-mann/84/9b7/100

Skype: rex.jones34
Twitter: @RexJonesII
Email: Rex.Jones@Test4Success.org
LinkedIn: https://www.linkedin.com/in/rexjones34

Copyright, Legal Notice, and Disclaimer

ISBN-13: 978-1530408368
ISBN-10: 1530408369

3 Tips To Master Selenium Within 30 Days
http://tinyurl.com/3-Tips-For-Selenium

Free Webinars, Videos, and Live Trainings
http://tinyurl.com/Free-QTP-UFT-Selenium

Acknowledgements

I would like to express my gratitude to my wife Tiffany, children Olivia Rexe' and Rex III, editor Samantha Mann, family, friends, and the many people who provided encouragement. Writing this book took time and your support helped pushed this book forward.

Thank You,

Rex Allen Jones II

Skype: rex.jones34
Twitter: @RexJonesII
Email: Rex.Jones@Test4Success.org
LinkedIn: https://www.linkedin.com/in/rexjones34

Videos

Building Blocks For Selenium

- (Part 1) Building Blocks For Selenium
  https://tinyurl.com/Selenium-Building-Blocks-Part1

- (Part 2) Building Blocks For Selenium
  https://tinyurl.com/Part2-Selenium-Building-Blocks

Java

- How To Install Selenium, Java, Eclipse, & TestNG
  https://tinyurl.com/Install-Selenium-Video

- Understanding Java Variables & Operators
  https://tinyurl.com/Variables-Operators-In-Java

Selenium

- Selenium Browser Methods
  https://tinyurl.com/BrowserMethods4Selenium

- Selenium WebElement Methods
  https://tinyurl.com/WebElementMethods4Selenium

Subscribe To Selenium 4 Beginners

- https://tinyurl.com/Subscribe-Selenium4Beginners

3 Tips To Master Selenium Within 30 Days
http://tinyurl.com/3-Tips-For-Selenium

Free Webinars, Videos, and Live Trainings
http://tinyurl.com/Free-QTP-UFT-Selenium

Chapter 1
Introduction to Java

Overview

Java is a powerful programming language developed by Sun Microsystems. It is a widely used object-oriented language that revolutionized the web. In addition to revolutionizing the web, Java is used in many devices, such as cell phones. The Java Development Kit (JDK) and one of the Integrated Development Environments (IDE), such as Eclipse, must be downloaded and installed in order to use Java. Steps for installing JDK and Eclipse are provided at the end of this chapter.

Once JDK and Eclipse IDE have been downloaded and installed, statements can be written and compiled. Statements are referred to as code—a line or lines of information written in a particular syntax. The key to all programming languages is the syntax. Syntax is a set of rules that specifies a structured combination of words and symbols. If not structured correctly, an error occurs to prevent the statements from compiling.

Compiling statements is performed via a compiler. A compiled language refers to a special program that retrieves the statements developed by a programmer and then translates the statements into an understandable machine language. A computer processor is then able to use the machine language once the statements are translated. It is important to know that comments are statements but ignored and never causes an error. Comments are notes that help programmers understand the program and/or other statements. The following are two types of comments:

1. Single line – comment one line at a time
2. Multi-line – comment multiple lines

Skype: rex.jones34
Twitter: @RexJonesII
Email: Rex.Jones@Test4Success.org
LinkedIn: https://www.linkedin.com/in/rexjones34

Chapter 1
Introduction to Java   (Part 1) Java 4 Selenium WebDriver

Usually, multi-line comments are located at the top of a program with information describing the entire program. Single line comments are used to explain statements within the program. The purpose of both types of comments is to self-document content written in the program. Comments provide answers to two questions:

1. What is the purpose of the program, statements, etc.?
2. Why did the programmer write the program, statements, etc.?

The following is an example of a single and multi-line comment:

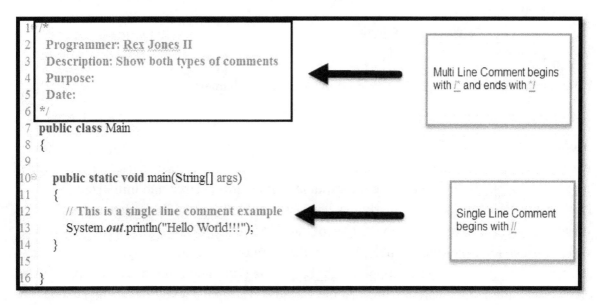

Figure 1.1 – Single and Multi-Line Examples

Program Output:
Hello World!!!

3 Tips To Master Selenium Within 30 Days
http://tinyurl.com/3-Tips-For-Selenium

Free Webinars, Videos, and Live Trainings
http://tinyurl.com/Free-QTP-UFT-Selenium

Line one begins the multi-line comment with a forward slash (/) and an asterisk (*) while line six ends the multi-line comment with an asterisk and forward slash (*/). Line 12 begins the single line comment with two forward slashes (//) and does not include symbols to end the comment.

This chapter provides general concepts regarding Java and will explain the following:

- ✓ Variables and Data Types
- ✓ Operators
- ✓ Control Structures
- ✓ Classes, Objects, and Methods
- ✓ Installations

<u>Note</u>: Details of the concepts are covered in subsequent chapters.

Variables and Data Types

A variable is a memory location with a name that contains a value (*see Variables and Data Types in Chapter 2*). In order to use the variable, it must be declared and initialized. Declaring a variable is stating clearly that a variable exists by providing a data type and variable name. Data type refers to the type of data that can be stored in a variable while variable name identifies the variable. In Java, there are two kinds of data types: primitive and reference. Primitive data type supports eight basic data types and reference data type is based on a class. Initializing a variable is when the variable is assigned a value that can change during program execution. The following is a variable declaration and initialization example:

Skype: rex.jones34
Twitter: @RexJonesII
Email: Rex.Jones@Test4Success.org
LinkedIn: https://www.linkedin.com/in/rexjones34

Chapter 1
Introduction to Java   (Part 1) Java 4 Selenium WebDriver

```
1   public class Declare_Initialize_Variable
2   {
3⊖     public static void main(String[] args)
4        {
5         int sum;

6
7         sum = 3 + 4;

8
9         System.out.println("What is the sum of 3 + 4? " + sum);
10      }
11  }
```

Variable Declaration
Data type = int
Variable Name = sum

Variable Initialization
sum = 3 + 4

Figure 1.2 – Variable Declaration and Initialization

Program Output:
What is the sum of 3 + 4? 7

Line five declares the variable with a data type "int" and variable name "sum" while line seven initializes "3 + 4" to the variable "sum". In Java, all variables possess a data type, variable name, and value.

Operators

Operators are symbols such as plus (+) and minus (-) that perform mathematical operations (*see Operators in Chapter 3*). The operators are executed on operands which is anything that can be changed. A variable is a common operand which changes during execution. In Java, there are four types of operators:

3 Tips To Master Selenium Within 30 Days
http://tinyurl.com/3-Tips-For-Selenium

Free Webinars, Videos, and Live Trainings
http://tinyurl.com/Free-QTP-UFT-Selenium

1. <u>Arithmetic</u> – implement mathematical operations on numerical values
2. <u>Bitwise</u> – work on operands utilizing bits
3. <u>Logical</u> – returns a boolean value (true or false) based on one or more expressions
4. <u>Relational</u> – returns a boolean value (true or false) after comparing operands

The following is an Arithmetic Operator example:

```
1  public class Subtraction_Operator
2  {
3      public static void main(String[] args)
4      {
5          // Subtraction Operator
6
7          int x, y, answer;
8
9          x = 100;
10         y = 80;
11
12         answer = x - y;
13         System.out.println("What is 100 - 80? " + answer);
14     }
15 }
```

The **Subtraction (-)** Operator is used to **subtract y from x**.

Figure 1.3 – Subtraction Arithmetic Operator

Program Output:
What is 100 - 80? 20

Line seven declares the variables "x, y, answer" with an <u>int</u> data type. However, lines nine and 10 assign the values (x = 100 and y = 80) to two of the variables. The <u>– Subtraction</u>

Skype: rex.jones34
Twitter: @RexJonesII
Email: Rex.Jones@Test4Success.org
LinkedIn: https://www.linkedin.com/in/rexjones34

Chapter 1
Introduction to Java   (Part 1) Java 4 Selenium WebDriver

operator is implemented at line 12 and subtracts the right underline operand "y" from the left underline operand "x" then assigns the value "20" to variable "answer".

Control Structures

Control structures provide ways to regulate the flow of a program (*see Control Structures in Chapter 4*). The flow is directed by branches and loops. Branches allow certain statements to be skipped after evaluating a condition or variable. Loops permit specific statements to be repeated according to a boolean expression. The following is a list of two branches and three loops:

Branches
1. If Branch – executes a statement when a condition is true
2. Switch Branch – evaluates a variable then execute a statement according to the variable's value

Loops
1. For Loop – executes a block of code a certain number of iterations
2. While Loop – repeats a statement while a boolean expression is true
3. Do While Loop – execute a statement at least one iteration and continue while the boolean expression is true

The following is an if branch example:

3 Tips To Master Selenium Within 30 Days
http://tinyurl.com/3-Tips-For-Selenium

Free Webinars, Videos, and Live Trainings
http://tinyurl.com/Free-QTP-UFT-Selenium

```
1   public class If_Branch
2   {
3       public static void main(String[] args)
4       {
5           // If Branch
6           boolean study;
7
8           study = true;
9
10          if (study == true)
11          {
12              System.out.println("You can learn Java / Selenium within 30 days");
13          }
14          else
15          {
16              System.out.println("May take a little longer than 30 days but remain patient");
17          }
18      }
19  }
```

> **If Branch** is evaluated by way of condition **(study == true)**. Line 12 is executed due to variable assigned value true in line 8.

Figure 1.4 – If Branch Example

Program Output:
```
You can learn Java / Selenium within 30 days
```

Line eight assigns variable "study" the value of true. As a result, the condition "if (study == true)" evaluates to true. Therefore, the program executes line 12 and skip the remaining lines (line 14 – 17). On the other hand, the program would have executed lines 14 – 17 and skipped lines 11 – 13 if the condition was false.

Skype: rex.jones34
Twitter: @RexJonesII
Email: Rex.Jones@Test4Success.org
LinkedIn: https://www.linkedin.com/in/rexjones34

Chapter 1
Introduction to Java   (Part 1) Java 4 Selenium WebDriver

Classes, Objects, and Methods

Java is an object-oriented programming (OOP) language that is structured around objects. An object is anything that can be seen or perceived. All objects have two characteristics: state and behavior. State identifies the object and behavior represent the actions of the object. For example, a customer can be identified by their name (state) while talking (behavior) is the action of the customer.

Both characteristics "state and behavior" are defined by a class. A class is a template for objects and forms the foundation for object-oriented programming. Data and statements that operate on the data are specified by classes. In addition, access to the data by way of classes are carried out through methods. A method manipulates data and provide interaction with classes from other components of the program. The following is an example illustrating a class, object, and method:

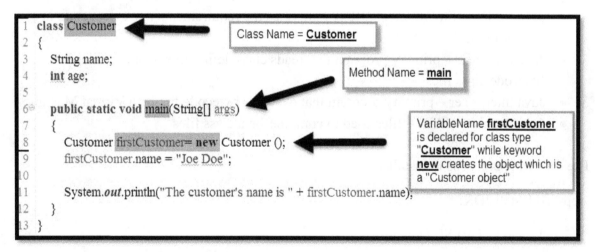

Figure 1.5 –Class, Object, and Method Example

Program Output:
The customer's name is Joe Doe

3 Tips To Master Selenium Within 30 Days
http://tinyurl.com/3-Tips-For-Selenium

Free Webinars, Videos, and Live Trainings
http://tinyurl.com/Free-QTP-UFT-Selenium

- Line one displays the keyword "class" and class name "Customer"
- Line six is a method labeled main
- Line eight declares firstCustomer as the variable for class type "Customer". Keyword "new" allocates memory and creates a new Customer object

Installations

Install Java Development Kit (JDK)

The Java Development Kit (JDK) is a software development environment used for writing code in Java. JDK includes many required components for creating and testing applications. Some of the components are Java Runtime Environment (JRE), Java Compiler, Java Interpreter, and Java Archiver (JAR).

- Java Runtime Environment (JRE) – provides the requirements to execute code in a web browser
- Java Compiler – primary program that reads class definitions then compiles it into bytecode class files
- Java Interpreter – primary program that executes bytecode for Java Virtual Machine
- Java Archiver (JAR) – files used to combine Java class files

The following are steps to install JDK:

Steps To Install JDK:

1. Go to Java SE Downloads
   http://www.oracle.com/technetwork/java/javase/downloads/index.html

Chapter 1
Introduction to Java   (Part 1) Java 4 Selenium WebDriver

2. Click the JDK Download button

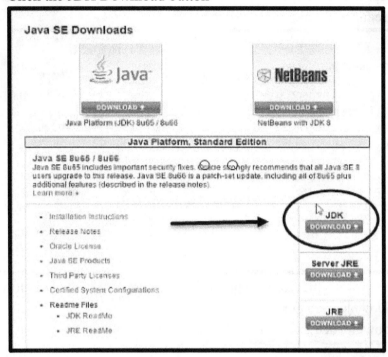

3. Click Accept License Agreement in the Java SE Development Kit 8u66 section
   Note: There may be a more recent version than 8u66

Java SE Development Kit 8u66

You must accept the Oracle Binary Code License Agreement for Java SE to download this software.

◯ Accept License Agreement ○ Decline License Agreement

Product / File Description	File Size	Download
Linux x86	154.67 MB	jdk-8u66-linux-i586.rpm
Linux x86	174.83 MB	jdk-8u66-linux-i586.tar.gz
Linux x64	152.69 MB	jdk-8u66-linux-x64.rpm
Linux x64	172.89 MB	jdk-8u66-linux-x64.tar.gz
Mac OS X x64	227.12 MB	jdk-8u66-macosx-x64.dmg
Solaris SPARC 64-bit (SVR4 package)	139.65 MB	jdk-8u66-solaris-sparcv9.tar.Z
Solaris SPARC 64-bit	99.05 MB	jdk-8u66-solaris-sparcv9.tar.gz
Solaris x64 (SVR4 package)	140 MB	jdk-8u66-solaris-x64.tar.Z
Solaris x64	96.2 MB	jdk-8u66-solaris-x64.tar.gz
Windows x86	181.33 MB	jdk-8u66-windows-i586.exe
Windows x64	186.65 MB	jdk-8u66-windows-x64.exe

4. Click the Download link for the appropriate System Type "i.e., Windows x64"
5. Go to the Download folder
6. Open the downloaded executable file

7. Click the Next button to Set Up Java SE Development Kit
8. Click the Next button for Custom Set Up
9. Click the Next button to Install to a specific location
   "i.e., C:\Program Files\Java"

10. Go to the location and Open the jdk folder "i.e., jdk1.8.0_66"

Skype: rex.jones34
Twitter: @RexJonesII
Email: Rex.Jones@Test4Success.org
LinkedIn: https://www.linkedin.com/in/rexjones34

Chapter 1
Introduction to Java   (Part 1) Java 4 Selenium WebDriver

11. Open the bin folder

12. Copy the bin folder's location "i.e., C:\Program Files\Java\jdk1.8.0_66\bin"

13. Access the Advanced system settings via <u>System</u>

14. Click the Advanced tab

15. Click Environment Variables

16. Go to Path within System variables section

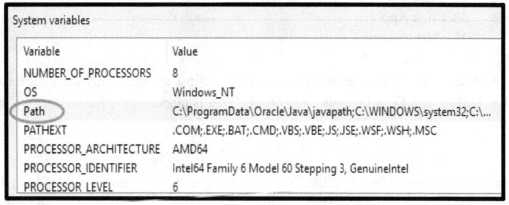

17. Click Edit

3 Tips To Master Selenium Within 30 Days
http://tinyurl.com/3-Tips-For-Selenium

Free Webinars, Videos, and Live Trainings
http://tinyurl.com/Free-QTP-UFT-Selenium

Chapter 1
Introduction to Java   (Part 1) Java 4 Selenium WebDriver

18. Paste the bin folder's location "i.e., C:\Program Files\Java\jdk1.8.0_66\bin"

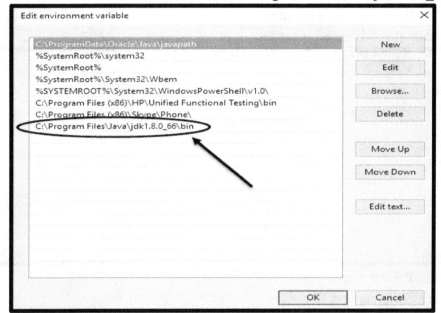

19. Click OK
20. Click Apply
21. Click OK

Note: Steps 10 – 21 are optional but beneficial. Eclipse automatically searches for the path "i.e., C:\Program Files\Java\jdk1.8.0_66\bin" that is placed in the Environment Variables modal.

Install Eclipse IDE

Eclipse is an open source IDE used for developing and testing applications. An IDE is comprehensive whereby it contains many features. The source code editor and debugger are some of the features. A source code editor allows code creation while a debugger examines the created code. Eclipse supports multiple programming languages but mainly used for Java.

Chapter 1
Introduction to Java   (Part 1) Java 4 Selenium WebDriver

One of the benefits of Eclipse is the use of plugins. The plugins allow customizations and additional functionalities. The following are steps to install Eclipse IDE:

Steps To Install Eclipse:

1. Go to https://eclipse.org/downloads/
2. Select the platform (Windows, Mac OS, or Linux)
3. Click the System Type "i.e., 64 bit" for Eclipse IDE for Java EE Developers

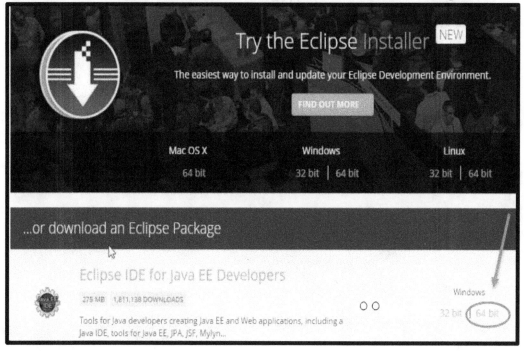

4. Choose a mirror close to you "i.e., Columbia University"

Choose a mirror close to you

North America

United States - **Columbia University**

5. Go to Download folder
6. Right click the Eclipse zip file and Extract All files

eclipse-jee-mars-1-win32-x86_64.zip

7. Open the eclipse.exe file to launch Eclipse IDE
    a. Go the extracted folder "i.e., eclipse-jee-mars-1-win32-x86_64"
    b. Open eclipse folder

Chapter 1
Introduction to Java   (Part 1) Java 4 Selenium WebDriver

c.   Right click eclipse.exe and Select Open

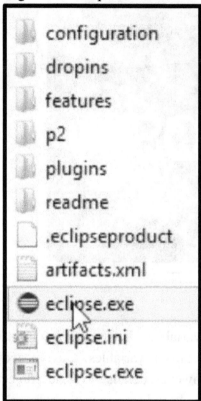

8. Load Eclipse IDE

Chapter 1 outlined general concepts regarding variables, data types, operators, control structures, classes, objects, and methods. The details of variables, data types, operators, and control structures are presented in this book. However, details of classes, objects, and methods are explained in the next book "(Part 2) Java 4 Selenium WebDriver" along with Object-Oriented Programming (OOP) concepts: Inheritance, Encapsulation, and Polymorphism. Chapter 2 will define the four types of variables local, parameter, instance, and class as well as primitive data types: boolean, byte, char, double, float, int, long, and short.

Chapter 2
Variables and Data Types

A variable is a named container or memory location that holds a value. The value of the container or memory location can change during execution of the program. Each variable has the ability to contain any kind of information, such as text or numbers. As a result, automation engineers are empowered to create flexible programs. Variables are utilized to represent changeable data, rather than hard-coding data (entering unchangeable data directly into a program).

All variables possess a name, data type, and value. A variable name is used to uniquely identify the variable. Data type refers to the type of variable, such as int, double, or boolean that can be stored in a variable. Therefore, data type determines a variable's value. In Java, there are two kinds of data types: primitive and reference. Primitive data type supports eight basic data types (explained in this chapter) and reference data type is based on a class (explained in Part 2 – Java 4 Selenium WebDriver).

Chapter two covers the following regarding variables and data types:

- ✓ Variable Names
- ✓ Variable Declaration
- ✓ Variable Initialization
- ✓ Variable Type, Scope, and Lifetime
- ✓ Primitive Data Types
- ✓ Constants

Variable Names

The name of a variable is significant when identifying the variable in memory. Hence, variables are referred to as identifiers. In addition to variables, an identifier represents methods along with other user-defined items. All variable names can range anywhere from one character to an unlimited number of characters. The following is a variable name example:

```
1  public class VariableExample
2  {
3      public static void main(String[] args)
4      {
5          int custOrder;
6
7          custOrder = 123;
8
9          System.out.println("The customer's order number is " + custOrder);
10     }
11 }
```

The variable name is **custOrder**

Figure 2.1 – Variable Name Example

Program Output:
```
The customer's order number is 123
```

Variable Naming Rules

Java has rules to naming variables. One of the rules is to ensure each variable has a unique name. Unique names prevent errors from occurring, such as "Duplicate local variable"—meaning the same variable name has been entered more than one time. The following is a list of more rules for naming a variable:

- Can contain case sensitive letters, numbers, dollar sign "$," and underscore "_"

Skype: rex.jones34
Twitter: @RexJonesII
Email: Rex.Jones@Test4Success.org
LinkedIn: https://www.linkedin.com/in/rexjones34

Chapter 2
Variables and Data Types   (Part 1) Java 4 Selenium WebDriver

- Can begin with a letter, dollar sign "$," or underscore "_"
- Cannot begin with a number
- Cannot contain a space or special character except dollar sign "$," and underscore "_"
- Cannot contain a reserve keyword

The following is a list of 50 Java reserve keywords:

abstract	continue	for	new	switch
assert	default	goto	package	synchronized
boolean	do	if	private	this
break	double	implements	protected	throw
byte	else	import	public	throws
case	enum	instanceof	return	transient
catch	extends	int	short	try
char	final	interface	static	void
class	finally	long	strictfp	volatile
const	float	native	super	while

Figure 2.2 - Reserve Keywords

Variable Naming Conventions

Convention is a general agreement or practice when establishing a standard. Suitable for naming variables, a convention is important while working with a team of automation engineers. All identifier names (e.g., variable, method, etc.) are critical for reading,

3 Tips To Master Selenium Within 30 Days
http://tinyurl.com/3-Tips-For-Selenium

Free Webinars, Videos, and Live Trainings
http://tinyurl.com/Free-QTP-UFT-Selenium

Chapter 2
Variables and Data Types   (Part 1) Java 4 Selenium WebDriver

understanding, and maintaining code. The following is a list of suggested conventions for naming a variable:

- Construct descriptive names that describe the variable's purpose
- Compose names utilizing mixed case letters, unless the name is one word
  - If one word, then use all lowercase letters
  - If multiple words, then begin the first word with a lowercase letter and each consecutive word with an uppercase letter (e.g., custFirstName)
- Create a name that begins with a letter and not a dollar sign "$" or underscore "_"
- Choose loop control variables that begin with a single lowercase letter (e.g., i, x, y)

Variable Declaration

Declaring a variable is stating clearly that a variable exists. All variables are associated with a data type in the event of declaring a variable. Data types guarantee the correct data is assigned to a variable. In addition, the size of a variable is determined by a data type. Variables must be declared before they are utilized in any program. The following is the syntax for declaring a variable:

 Syntax
variableType variableName;

Syntax Details

Argument	Description
variableType	Data type of variable being declared
variableName	Name of variable being declared
;	Semi-colon completes the declaration statement

Skype: rex.jones34
Twitter: @RexJonesII
Email: Rex.Jones@Test4Success.org
LinkedIn: https://www.linkedin.com/in/rexjones34

Chapter 2
Variables and Data Types   (Part 1) Java 4 Selenium WebDriver

Figure 2.3 – Variable Declaration Syntax Details

The following is a variable declaration example:

```
1  public class VariableExample
2  {
3      public static void main(String[] args)
4      {
5          int x;
6          int y;
7
8          x = 5;
9          y = 7;
10
11         System.out.println("The values of x and y are: " + x + " and " + y);
12     }
13 }
```

The data type is **int** while **x** and **y** are the variable names

Figure 2.4 – Variable Declaration

Program Output:
The values of x and y are: 5 and 7

Lines five and six declare variables x and y with an int data type. Notice how each declaration ends with a semi-colon. The semi-colon completes the declaration statement.

Note: Multiple variables can be declared on the same line if the variable has the same data type. The following is a declaration example of multiple variables separated by a comma:

int x, y;

3 Tips To Master Selenium Within 30 Days
http://tinyurl.com/3-Tips-For-Selenium

Free Webinars, Videos, and Live Trainings
http://tinyurl.com/Free-QTP-UFT-Selenium

Variable Initialization

In general, variables are given an initial value before the variables are used. The Assignment Operator separates two sides of an equation. There is a left and right side of every equation. The left side displays a variable name while the right side displays a value. Variables can be initialized the following ways:

1. Initialize by Value
2. Initialize by Dynamics

Initialize by Value

Initializing a variable by values requires a value to be set for the variable. The following are two ways to initialize a variable by value:

1. At declaration
2. After declaration

At declaration

At declaration is when the data type, variable name, and value are placed on the same line. In other words, the variable is declared and initialized simultaneously. Multiple variables can be initialized at declaration by using a comma separated list. The following is an example of "at declaration" initialize by value:

Chapter 2
Variables and Data Types   (Part 1) Java 4 Selenium WebDriver

```
1   public class VariableExample
2   {
3⊖      public static void main(String[] args)
4       {
5           int num1 = 100, num2 = 200, total;
6
7           total = num1 + num2;
8
9           System.out.println("The total of num1 and num2 is " + total);
10      }
11  }
```

Variables **num1** and **num2** are initialized by values **100** and **200** within the same statement

Figure 2.5 – Variable Initialization At Declaration

Program Output:

```
The total of num1 and num2 is 300
```

Line five declares three variables "num1, num2, and total" with an int data type. Two of the variables "num1 and num2" are initialized with a value that represents variable initialization at declaration. Therefore, the variables are initialized when they are declared.

After declaration

After declaration is when the data type, variable name, and value are placed on two separate lines. The data type and variable name are declared on the same line while the variable name is assigned a value on a subsequent line. The following is an example of "after declaration" initialize by value:

3 Tips To Master Selenium Within 30 Days
http://tinyurl.com/3-Tips-For-Selenium

Free Webinars, Videos, and Live Trainings
http://tinyurl.com/Free-QTP-UFT-Selenium

```
1   public class VariableExample
2   {
3⊖    public static void main(String[] args)
4     {
5        int num1, num2, total;
6
7        num1 = 100;
8        num2 = 200;
9
10       total = num1 + num2;
11
12       System.out.println("The total of num1 and num2 is " + total);
13    }
14 }
```

Variables **num1** and **num2** are initialized by values **100** and **200** on separate statements

Figure 2.6 – Variable Initialization After Declaration

Program Output:
```
The total of num1 and num2 is 300
```

Line five declares three variables "num1, num2, and total" with an _int_ data type. Two of the variables "num1 and num2" are initialized with a value on lines seven and eight that represents variable initialization after declaration. Therefore, the variables are declared on line five and initialized after they are declared on lines seven and eight.

Initialize by Dynamics

Initializing a variable by dynamics does not assign a specific value to a variable. Instead, values subject to change are assigned to the variables. Occasionally, values that change are values from an Application Under Test (AUT) or other variables. The following is a variable initialization by dynamics example:

Chapter 2
Variables and Data Types   (Part 1) Java 4 Selenium WebDriver

```
1  public class VariableExample
2  {
3      public static void main(String[] args)
4      {
5          int num1, num2;
6
7          num1 = 100;
8          num2 = 200;
9
10         int total = num1 + num2;
11
12         System.out.println("The total of num1 and num2 is " + total);
13     }
14 }
```

Variable **total** is initialized dynamically via expression **num1 + num2**

Figure 2.7 – Initialize by Dynamics

Program Output:
The total of num1 and num2 is 300

Line 10 declares and initializes variable "total" with an int data type. The variable is not initialized with a specific value. However, the variable is initialized with information "num1 and num2" that can possibly change during execution. For example, an automation engineer can enter statements to increase the value of both variables "num1 and num2" during execution. If variables num1 and num2 change, then the variable "total" will dynamically change.

Note: Line 10 requires a data type int when initializing a variable by dynamics.

Variable Type, Scope, and Lifetime

Java allows a variable to be declared anywhere in a program. For that reason, a variable can be defined within a class, within a method, or within a method as a parameter. A variable's scope is related to where the variable is declared inside the program. Lifetime is how long the variable exists in the program. The following are four types of variables that have their own scope and lifetime:

1. Local Variables
2. Parameter Variables
3. Instance Variables
4. Class Variables

Local Variables

Local variables are declared inside a method. Individual methods can have the same variable name as another method within a program. Local variables are only visible inside its individual method. Therefore, each variable is unique to a specific method. Before using a local variable, it must be declared and initialized a value without needing a special keyword. Hence, there are no default values for local variables. Local variables are created when the method is constructed and destroyed when the method is terminated. The following is a local variable example:

Chapter 2
Variables and Data Types   (Part 1) Java 4 Selenium WebDriver

```
 1  public class VariableExample
 2  {
 3      public void AutomationEngineers ()
 4      {
 5          int yearsEmployed;
 6
 7          yearsEmployed = 5;
 8
 9          System.out.println("Joe Doe 'Automation' has been at the organization " + yearsEmployed + " years");
10      }
11      public void Developers ()
12      {
13          int yearsEmployed;
14
15          yearsEmployed = 3;
16
17          System.out.println("Jane Doe 'Dev' has been at the organization " + yearsEmployed + " years");
18      }
19      public static void main(String[] args)
20      {
21          VariableExample years = new VariableExample ();
22          years.AutomationEngineers();
23          years.Developers();
24      }
25  }
```

Local variable **yearsEmployed** within method **AutomationEngineers**

Local variable **yearsEmployed** within method **Developers**

Figure 2.8 – Local Variable

Program Output:
```
Joe Doe 'Automation' has been at the organization 5 years
Jane Doe 'Dev' has been at the organization 3 years
```

Lines five and thirteen display a variable "yearsEmployed" that is local to methods "AutomationEngineers and Developers." An error will not occur because each variable is unique to its method. However, the same variable name cannot be declared multiple times

3 Tips To Master Selenium Within 30 Days
http://tinyurl.com/3-Tips-For-Selenium

Free Webinars, Videos, and Live Trainings
http://tinyurl.com/Free-QTP-UFT-Selenium

within the same method. The scope and lifetime of a local variable is limited to the block/curly braces in which it is declared.

Parameter Variables

Parameter variables are declared and passed into methods. After a parameter variable is declared, it is implemented like a local variable. Therefore, a local variable and parameter variable cannot have the same name. Keywords are not required for a parameter variable. However, the data type and variable name must be surrounded by a parenthesis after the method name. The following is a parameter variable example:

```
1   public class VariableExample
2   {
3       public void setMtgAmount (double mtgAmount)        ◄──────
4       {
5           System.out.println("The mortgage payment amount is " + mtgAmount);
6       }
7
8       public static void main String[] args)            ◄──────
9       {
10          VariableExample payment = new VariableExample ();
11          payment.setMtgAmount(99000);
12      }
13  }
```

Variables **double mtgAmount** and **String[] args** are declared within a method as a parameter

Figure 2.9 – Parameter Variables

Program Output:
```
The mortgage payment amount is 99000.0
```

Lines three and eight pass parameter variables "double mtgAmount and String[] args" into methods "setMtgAmount and main." The value "99000" is passed from the method call "payment.setMtgAmount" line 11 into the method "setMtgAmount" line three that is called. The scope of a parameter variable is a method's header inside the parenthesis while the lifetime is a method's body within the curly brackets.

Skype: rex.jones34
Twitter: @RexJonesII
Email: Rex.Jones@Test4Success.org
LinkedIn: https://www.linkedin.com/in/rexjones34

Chapter 2
Variables and Data Types

(Part 1) Java 4 Selenium WebDriver

Instance Variables

Instance variables are declared inside a <u>class</u>, outside of a <u>method</u>, and can be optionally accessed after creating an <u>object</u>. The values of an instance variable are unique to each <u>object</u>. Instance variable can be declared before or after it is initialized with visibility to all <u>methods</u> in a <u>class</u>. Default values for a number is zero, for <u>boolean</u> the default is false, and an object reference default is null. The following is an instance variable example:

```
1  public class VariableExample
2  {
3      int yearsExist = 34;
4
5      public static void main(String[] args)
6      {
7          VariableExample years = new VariableExample ();
8          System.out.println("This organization has existed for " + years.yearsExist + " years");
9      }
10 }
```

Instance variable **yearsExist** declared in class **VariableExample** but outside of method **main.** The instance variable is accessed after creating object **years**

Figure 2.10 – Instance Variable

Program Output:
```
This organization has existed for 34 years
```

Line three declares the instance variable "yearsExist" within the class "VariableExample," but outside of the <u>method</u> "main". The instance variable is accessed in line eight "years.yearsExist" after creating keyword <u>new</u> via line seven.

Note: An instance variable can be accessed directly by calling the instance variable. However in this example, the instance variable is accessed via ObjectReference due to the static method starting at line five. Line eight prints the variable's value by using the ObjectReference.InstanceVariable "years.yearsExist".

3 Tips To Master Selenium Within 30 Days
http://tinyurl.com/3-Tips-For-Selenium

Free Webinars, Videos, and Live Trainings
http://tinyurl.com/Free-QTP-UFT-Selenium

Class Variables

Class Variables (known as Static Variables) are declared in a class, but not in a method. This type of variable is declared using keyword static. The keyword static announces to the compiler that only one copy of a particular variable exists, but is shared by all instances of an object. Default values for a number is zero, the default for boolean is false, and an object reference default is null. Class Variables are created when the program begins and destroyed when the program ends. The following is a class variable example:

```
1  public class VariableExample
2  {
3      static int numDays = 30;
4
5      public static void main(String[] args)
6      {
7          VariableExample days = new VariableExample ();
8          System.out.println("Java can be mastered in  " + VariableExample.numDays + " days");
9          System.out.println("Selenium can be mastered in " + days.numDays + " days");
10         System.out.println("Do you think you can master Java/Selenium in " + numDays + " days");
11     }
12 }
```

Class variable **numDays** was declared within class VariableExample but outside method **main**. It can be assessed via class name **VariableExample**, object reference **days,** or class variable name **numDays**

Figure 2.11 – Class Variable

Program Output:
```
Java can be mastered in  30 days
Selenium can be mastered in 30 days
```

Line three declares the Class Variable "numDays" within the class "VariableExample," but outside of the method "main." The scope of a class variable is inside the block/curly braces of class and outside the block/curly braces of all methods. Therefore, the lifetime of the variable continues throughout execution of the program.

Note: A class variable can be accessed via ClassName, ObjectReference, or ClassVariableName. If accessed by way of Object Reference then keyword "new" must be created. Lines eight, nine, and ten access the class variable by using the ClassName.ClassVariable "VariableExample.numDays", ObjectReference.ClassVariable "days.numDays", and ClassVariableName "numDays".

Primitive Data Types

The primitive data types give an account for the type of data that is stored in a variable. Each data type has a precise range and behavior. Consequently, a data type of int can store numerical data, but a type mismatch error will occur if boolean attempts to store numerical data. In addition, certain operations are permitted on values depending on the data type. As an example, a math calculation cannot be performed on a boolean data type because a boolean cannot contain numbers. The following is a list of all eight primitive data types:

Type	Width in Bits (Bytes)	Description/Range
boolean		True or False values
byte	8-bit (1-byte)	-128 to 127
char	16-bit	Standard character set that can be a letter, control character, number, punctuation, or symbol representing all languages in the world
double	64-bit (8-byte)	-1.7976931348623157E+308 to 1.7976931348623157E+308
float	32-bit (4-byte)	-3.4028235E+38 to 3.4028235E+38
int	32-bit (4-byte)	−2,147,483,648 to 2,147,483,647

| long | 64-bit (8-byte) | -9,223,372,036,854,775,808 to 9,223,372,036,854,755,807 |
| short | 16-bit (2-byte) | -32,768 to 32,767 |

Figure 2.12 – Eight Primitive Data Types

The following divides the primitive data types into 4 categories:

1. Integer Type
2. Floating Point Type
3. Character Type
4. Boolean Type

Integer Type

The integer type supports numerical values without a fractional component. A major difference within the integer type is the range of values. The following show each data type for integer type:

- byte
- short
- int
- long

Data type int is used the most because it is used for controlling loops and indexing arrays. The following is an int data type example:

Skype: rex.jones34
Twitter: @RexJonesII
Email: Rex.Jones@Test4Success.org
LinkedIn: https://www.linkedin.com/in/rexjones34

Chapter 2
Variables and Data Types   (Part 1) Java 4 Selenium WebDriver

```
 1  public class VariableExample
 2  {
 3      public static void main(String[] args)
 4      {
 5          // Calculate 2 integer values
 6          int i, j;
 7          int total;
 8
 9          i = 10;
10          j = 20;
11          total = i + j;
12
13          System.out.println ("Total of i + j is " + total);
14      }
15  }
```

Data Type int

Figure 2.13 – Data Type int

Program Output:
Total of i + j is 30

Lines six and seven declare an <u>int</u> data type for names "i," "j," and "total." Lines nine, ten, and eleven initialize the variables.

Floating Point Type

The floating point type supports numerical values with a fractional component. Data types float and double make up the floating point type category. Due to Java's standard Math class, the double data type is used the most when a numerical value includes a fraction. The following is a double data type example:

3 Tips To Master Selenium Within 30 Days
http://tinyurl.com/3-Tips-For-Selenium

Free Webinars, Videos, and Live Trainings
http://tinyurl.com/Free-QTP-UFT-Selenium

```
1   public class VariableExample
2   {
3⊖      public static void main(String[] args)
4       {
5           double d;
6           double calc;
7
8           d = 200;
9           calc = Math.sqrt (d);
10
11          System.out.println ("Square root of 200 is " + calc);
12      }
13  }
```

Data Type double

Figure 2.14 – Data Type double

Program Output:
```
Square root of 200 is 14.142135623730951
```

Lines five and six declare a double data type for names "d" and "calc." Line eight assigns 200 to variable "d", while line nine assigns a square root method to variable "calc." The "sqrt ()" method is a method within the standard Math class which returns a double data type.

Character Type

The character type supports a Unicode system that displays all characters for every human language. In order to represent all characters, the char data type holds a 16-bit type that has a range of 0 to 65,535. The range helps Unicode assign every letter, number, and symbol an exclusive numerical value. The following is a char data type example:

Skype: rex.jones34
Twitter: @RexJonesII
Email: Rex.Jones@Test4Success.org
LinkedIn: https://www.linkedin.com/in/rexjones34

Chapter 2
Variables and Data Types   (Part 1) Java 4 Selenium WebDriver

```
1   public class VariableExample
2   {
3⊖     public static void main(String[] args)
4       {
5           char cha1, cha2;                    ⬅     Data Type char
6
7           cha1 = 'C';
8           cha2 = 67;
9
10          System.out.println("Value assigned to cha1 is " + cha1);
11          System.out.println("67 is the Unicode for " + cha2);
12      }
13  }
```

Figure 2.15 – Data Type char

Program Output:
```
Value assigned to cha1 is C
67 is the Unicode for C
```

Line five declares a char data type for names "cha1" and "cha2." Lines seven assigns the letter 'C', utilizing single quotes while line eight assigns a value of 67. Constants such as line seven declared with a char data type always use a single quote (') for a letter. Value 67 is the American Standard Code for Information Interchange (ASCII) for the letter 'C'.

Note: According to webopedia, "ASCII is a code for representing English characters as numbers, with each letter assigned a number from 0 to 127".

3 Tips To Master Selenium Within 30 Days
http://tinyurl.com/3-Tips-For-Selenium

Free Webinars, Videos, and Live Trainings
http://tinyurl.com/Free-QTP-UFT-Selenium

Boolean Type

The boolean type supports a program when the program involves logic. Thus, the boolean data type returns a value after evaluating a logical/conditional statement. Conditional statements require an answer (true or false) regarding a specific statement. A conditional statement consists of variables and/or expressions. The following is a boolean data type example:

```
1  public class VariableExample
2  {
3    public static void main(String[] args)
4    {
5      boolean result;              <---   Data Type boolean
6
7      result = false;
8
9      System.out.println("Boolean variable 'result' was initialized to " + result);
10     System.out.println("Is this a true or false statement '100 greater than 99'? " + (100>99));
11   }
12 }
```

Figure 2.16 – Data Type boolean

Program Output:
```
Boolean variable 'result' was initialized to false
Is this a true or false statement '100 greater than 99'? true
```

Line five declares a boolean data type for variable "result." Line seven initializes false to the variable. Line nine prints the default value of false, but line ten return a true value after evaluating condition "100>99." True is returned because 100 is greater than 99.

Skype: rex.jones34
Twitter: @RexJonesII
Email: Rex.Jones@Test4Success.org
LinkedIn: https://www.linkedin.com/in/rexjones34

Constants

Constants (also known as Literals) are unchangeable values assigned to a variable name of a particular data type. The way each Constant is defined depends upon its data type. Defining a Constant is a defense mechanism to protect information so that the value remains fixed. For instance, the total hours in a day is 24, therefore, a Constant is declared so that the value of 24 does not change. The following are four types of constants:

1. String Constants
2. Character Constants
3. Boolean Constants
4. Numeric Constants

Constant Naming Conventions

A standard naming convention for Constants facilitate the process of locating the Constants. The following are Constant naming conventions:

- Construct descriptive names that describe the Constant's purpose
- Create a name that includes all capital letters (e.g., CUSTOMER)
- Compose a name utilizing all capital letters with an underscore if the name consists of multiple words (e.g., ORDER_NUM)

Declare and Initialize Constants

Constants are declared and initialized similar to variables. The distinguishing characteristic of declaring a Constant is the keyword modifier final. A declaration statement utilizing final informs Java that the initialization value will not be changed. The following example shows a constant declaration and initialization statement:

```
1  public class ConstantExamples
2  {
3      public static void main(String[] args)
4      {
5          //Declare the number of days and hours using a constant
6          final int DAYS_IN_WEEK = 7;
7          final int DAILY_MAX_HOURS = 24;
8          int totalHours;
9
10         totalHours = DAYS_IN_WEEK * DAILY_MAX_HOURS;
11
12         System.out.println("The total of hours in a week is " + totalHours);
13      }
14 }
```

Constant Declaration and Initialization using the keyword modifier **final**

Figure 2.17 – Declare and Initialize Constants

Program Output:
The total of hours in a week is 168

Lines six and seven declare and initialize Constants using keyword modifier final. Constant name DAYS_IN_WEEK assigned "7", while DAILY_MAX_HOURS assigned "24". The assigned Constant values will not change in the program. An error states "The final local variable NAME_OF_CONSTANT cannot be assigned" if there is an attempt to change a Constant.

Default Constant Data Types

Data types int and double are default Constant types in their respective category. However, the default type can be modified by appending a letter of the target type. An int data type changes to a long data type by attaching the letter "l" or "L." For example, a value of 34 indicates an int data type by default but 34l or 34L indicates a long data type. The same is true with a <u>double</u> data type. A value of 12.34 specifies a <u>double</u> data type by default, but 12.34f or 12.34F specifies a <u>float</u> data type.

<u>Note</u>: This section points out the default constant data types. However, a constant can be declared as any <u>primitive data type</u>.

Escape Characters

Escape characters (known as backslash character constants) represent a group of characters and non-graphical characters. According to Beginning Java® Programming (2015), "escape characters are used for displaying text in specific ways, either for inserting tabs or enters where desired, or by displaying a character that's normally reserved for code syntax" (page 29).

Characters such as single quotes ('') have a distinct meaning and cannot be used directly. Therefore, a backslash character (\) must precede the character so that the <u>compiler</u> interprets a given statement correctly. The following is a list of escape characters:

Escape Character	Description	Unicode
\b	Inserts a backspace in the text	\u0008
\f	Inserts a form feed in the text	\u000C
\n	Inserts a new line feed in the text	\u000A
\r	Inserts a carriage return in the text	\u000D
\t	Inserts a horizontal tab in the text	\u0009
\'	Inserts a single quote (apostrophe) in the text	\u0027
\"	Inserts a double quote in the text	\u0022

3 Tips To Master Selenium Within 30 Days
http://tinyurl.com/3-Tips-For-Selenium

Free Webinars, Videos, and Live Trainings
http://tinyurl.com/Free-QTP-UFT-Selenium

\\	Inserts a backslash in the text	\u005C

Figure 2.18 – Escape Characters

String Constants

String Constants are enclosed in double quotes ("") representing a sequence of characters. Regular characters (e.g., numbers, letters, etc.), as well as escape characters, can be processed in a String Constant. The following is a Sting Constant example:

```
1  public class MiscExamples
2  {
3      public static void main(String[] args)
4      {
5          System.out.print("The following displays numbers 1 - 10 on two lines: \n");
6          System.out.println("1\t2\t3\t4\t5");
7          System.out.println("6\t7\t8\t9\t10");
8      }
9  }
10
```

String literals are located within the double quotes

Figure 2.19 – String Constant Example

Program Output:
```
The following displays numbers 1 - 10 on two lines:
1      2      3      4      5
6      7      8      9      10
```

Lines five, six, and seven display String Constants within the double quotes. Notice how line five has a print () statement rather println () statement like lines six and seven. The escape character (\n) inserts a new line feed so println () is not needed. In addition, escape character (\t) is used in lines six and seven to insert a tab between numbers 1 through 10.

Chapter 2
Variables and Data Types   (Part 1) Java 4 Selenium WebDriver

Character Constants

Character Constants are always initialized in single quotes ('') and hold only one character. Figure 2.15 is char example initializing the letter 'C' to a variable named cha1 in line seven. The single quotes apply to letters and not numbers assigned to Character Constants.

Boolean Constants

Boolean Constants initializes True and False values. Figure 2.16 is a boolean example initializing a True value to a variable named "result" in line seven.

Numeric Constants

Numeric Constants contain integer type or floating point type values. These values allow underscores (_) to be used like a punctuation mark. Usually, a comma, hyphen (-), etc. divides a numerical value containing several digits. For instance, one hundred million is written as 100,000,000. The commas improve readability of hundred million similar to an underscore improving a Numeric Constant. The following is a Numeric Constant example displaying multiple underscores for a similar value:

```
1  public class MiscExamples
2  {
3    public static void main(String[] args)
4    {
5      final long FIRST_AMOUNT, SECOND_AMOUNT, TOTAL_AMOUNT;
6
7      FIRST_AMOUNT = 111_111_111;
8      SECOND_AMOUNT = 222222222;
9
10     TOTAL_AMOUNT = FIRST_AMOUNT + SECOND_AMOUNT;
11
12     System.out.println("The first amount is " + FIRST_AMOUNT);
13     System.out.println("The second amount is " + SECOND_AMOUNT);
14     System.out.println("The total of both amounts is " + TOTAL_AMOUNT);
15   }
16 }
```

A long data type displaying several numbers can optionally use underscores to make values (e.g., **111_111_111**) readable

Figure 2.20 – Numeric Constant Example

Program Output:
```
The first amount is 111111111
The second amount is 222222222
The total of both amounts is 333333333
```

Lines seven and eight display a long data type containing nine digits in their value. However, line seven displays two underscores to make the value 111_111_111 more readable than line eight displaying value 222222222. To the same extent, an underscore can be used for credit card numbers, social security numbers, etc. and can only be placed between digits.

Chapter 2 described how to declare and initialize variables. In addition, the four types of variables (local, parameter, instance, and class) and primitive data types were discussed. Chapter 3 will explore the four types of Java operators: Arithmetic, Bitwise, Logical, and Relational.

Chapter 3
Operators

Operators are symbols that perform mathematical or logical manipulations on one or more operands. An operand is anything that can be changed or manipulated. The most common type of operand is a variable. In Java, there are four types of operators: <u>Arithmetic</u>, <u>Bitwise</u>, <u>Logical</u>, and <u>Relational</u>. <u>Arithmetic</u>, <u>Logical</u>, and <u>Relational</u> operators are the most used operators. The following example demonstrates a <u>Multiplication (*)</u> Operator and operands (three and four):

```
1  public class Operators
2  {
3      public static void main(String[] args)
4      {
5          int answer;
6
7          answer = 3 * 4;
8
9          System.out.println("What is 3 times 4? " + answer);
10     }
11 }
```

The operands are **3** and **4** while the multiplication symbol (*) is the operator

Figure 3.1 – Operator and Operands

Program Output:
What is 3 times 4? 12

3 Tips To Master Selenium Within 30 Days
http://tinyurl.com/3-Tips-For-Selenium

Free Webinars, Videos, and Live Trainings
http://tinyurl.com/Free-QTP-UFT-Selenium

Chapter 3
Operators

(Part 1) Java 4 Selenium WebDriver

This chapter provides the following information regarding operators:

- ✓ Arithmetic Operators
- ✓ Bitwise Operators
- ✓ Logical Operators
- ✓ Relational Operators
- ✓ Assignment Operator
- ✓ Ternary Operator
- ✓ Operator Precedence
- ✓ Data Type Casting
- ✓ Expressions

Arithmetic Operators

Arithmetic operators implement mathematical operations on numerical values. Therefore, the arithmetic operators can be applied to any data type involving numbers. The following is a list of arithmetic operators:

1. + (Addition) operator
2. - (Subtraction) operator
3. * (Multiplication) operator
4. / (Division) operator
5. % (Modulus) operator
6. ++ (Increment) operator
7. -- (Decrement) operator

Operator	Description
+	Adds a value on both sides of the (+) operator Used for joining strings which is known as string concatenation

Skype: rex.jones34
Twitter: @RexJonesII
Email: Rex.Jones@Test4Success.org
LinkedIn: https://www.linkedin.com/in/rexjones34

(Part 1) Java 4 Selenium WebDriver

-	Subtracts right operand from left operand
*	Multiplies values on both sides of the (*) operand
/	Divides left operand by right operand
%	Divides left operand by right operand then returns the remainder
++	Increases the operand's value by one
--	Decreases the operand's value by one

Figure 3.2 – Arithmetic Operators

<u>Note</u>: The Division Operator (/) truncates the remainder while the Modulus Operator (%) returns the remainder. For instance, 10/3 only returns three and truncates the remainder, which is one. On the other hand, 10%3 only returns the remainder of one.

Increment Arithmetic Operator

The Increment Operator adds one to an <u>operand</u>. This operator has a prefix and postfix form. The below syntaxes show both increment operator forms which is the same as the following expression:

i = i + 1;

Prefix Form Syntax
++i;

Postfix Form Syntax
i++;

Decrement Arithmetic Operator

The Decrement Operator subtracts one from an operand. This operator has a prefix and postfix form. The below syntaxes show both decrement operator forms which is the same as the following expression:

i = i - 1;

Prefix Form Syntax
--i;

Postfix Form Syntax
i--;

The following are examples of each arithmetic operator:

Skype: rex.jones34
Twitter: @RexJonesII
Email: Rex.Jones@Test4Success.org
LinkedIn: https://www.linkedin.com/in/rexjones34

Chapter 3
Operators

(Part 1) Java 4 Selenium WebDriver

```
1   public class Operators
2   {
3       public static void main(String[] args)
4       {
5           int result, x = 10, y = 3;
6
7           result = x + y;  // Addition
8           System.out.println("What is 10 plus 3? " + result);
9
10          result = x - y;  // Subtraction
11          System.out.println("What is 10 minus 3? " + result);
12
13          result = x * y;  // Multiplication
14          System.out.println("What is 10 times 3? " + result);
15
16          result = x / y;  // Division
17          System.out.println("What is 10 divided 3? " + result);
18
19          result = x % y;  // Modulus
20          System.out.println("What is the remainder of 10 divided 3? " + result);
21
22          result = ++x;  // Prefix Increment
23          System.out.println("What is the prefix increment value of 10? " + result);
24
25          result = x++;  // Postfix Increment
26          System.out.println("What is the postfix increment value of 10? " + result);
27
28          result = --y;  // Prefix Decrement
29          System.out.println("What is the prefix decrement value of 3? " + result);
30
31          result = y--;  // Postfix Decrement
32          System.out.println("What is the postfix decrement value of 3? " + result);
33      }
34  }
```

Figure 3.3 – Arithmetic Operator Examples

3 Tips To Master Selenium Within 30 Days
http://tinyurl.com/3-Tips-For-Selenium

Free Webinars, Videos, and Live Trainings
http://tinyurl.com/Free-QTP-UFT-Selenium

Program Output:
```
What is 10 plus 3? 13
What is 10 minus 3? 7
What is 10 times 3? 30
What is 10 divided 3? 3
What is the remainder of 10 divided 3? 1
What is the prefix increment value of 10? 11
What is the postfix increment value of 10? 11
What is the prefix decrement value of 3? 2
What is the postfix decrement value of 3? 2
```

In this example, line five declares and initializes the variables. Variable "x" is assigned 10 while "y" is assigned three. An + (Addition) operator adds both variables in line seven. Variable "result" is assigned the sum of variables "x" and "y" which results in 13. A similar process is performed for all examples in Figure 3.3 using a different Arithmetic Operator according to Figure 3.2.

Bitwise Operators

The Bitwise Operator work on operands utilizing bits. Therefore this operator have a foundation that functions on a bit-by-bit basis. Values are made available after the bits are set, shifted, and tested. Primarily, the Bitwise Operators are used on data types byte, char, int, long, and short. The following is a list of bitwise operators and examples:

1. & (Bitwise AND) operator
2. | (Bitwise OR) operator
3. ^ (Bitwise exclusive OR (XOR)) operator
4. >> (Signed shift right) operator
5. >>> (Unsigned shift right) operator
6. << (Signed shift left) operator
7. ~ (One's Compliment) operator

Skype: rex.jones34
Twitter: @RexJonesII
Email: Rex.Jones@Test4Success.org
LinkedIn: https://www.linkedin.com/in/rexjones34

Operator	Description	Example
&	Places 1 bit in the result if a bit exists in both operands. Can be used on a boolean data type	x & y;
|	Places 1 bit in the result if a bit exists in one of both operands. Can be used on a boolean data type	x | y;
^	Places 1 bit in the result if a bit exists in one of the operands (not both)	x ^ y:
>>	Shifts the left operand's value to the right by the number of bits specified by the right operand	x >> 2
>>>	Shifts the left operand's value to the right by the number of bits specified by the right operand while shifted value are filled with zeros (0)	x >>> 2
<<	Shifts the left operand's value to the left by the number of bits specified by the right operand	x << 2
~	Changes every bit to the opposite bit. For example, every 1 bit changes to 0 and every 0 bit changes to 1	~2

Figure 3.4 – Bitwise Operators

Logical Operators

Logical Operators (known as Conditional Operators) return a boolean value based on one or more expressions. Therefore, the Logical Operator's data type must be boolean. The following is a list of logical operators:

- && (Logical AND) operator
- || (Logical OR) operator
- ^ (Logical exclusive OR (XOR)) operator

- ! (Logical NOT) operator

Operator	Description
&&	Returns true if both operands are true Returns false if one operand or both operands are false
||	Returns true if one operand or both operands are true Returns false if both operands are false
^	Returns true if only one operand is true Returns false if both operands are false and if both operands are true
!	Returns the opposite value of the operand Returns true if the operand is false and return false if the operand is true

Figure 3.5 – Logical Operators

Note: The Bitwise Operators and Logical Operators perform some of the same functions. The following are examples of each logical operator and two bitwise operators:

Skype: rex.jones34
Twitter: @RexJonesII
Email: Rex.Jones@Test4Success.org
LinkedIn: https://www.linkedin.com/in/rexjones34

Chapter 3
Operators   (Part 1) Java 4 Selenium WebDriver

```
 1  public class Operators
 2  {
 3      public static void main (String[] args)
 4      {
 5          boolean x = 100 > 99, y = 99 > 100;
 6
 7          // Logical AND '&&' operator
 8          System.out.println("What is the result of 100 > 99 && 99 > 100? " + (x && y));
 9
10          // Bitwise AND '&' operator
11          System.out.println("What is the result of 100 > 99 & 99 > 100? " + (x & y));
12
13          // Logical OR '||' operator
14          System.out.println("What is the result of 100 > 99 || 99 > 100? " + (x || y));
15
16          // Bitwise OR '|' operator
17          System.out.println("What is the result of 100 > 99 | 99 > 100? " + (x | y));
18
19          // Logical XOR '^' operator
20          System.out.println("What is the result of 100 > 99 ^ 99 > 100? " + (x ^ y));
21
22          // Logical NOT '!' operator
23          System.out.println("What is the result of Not 100 > 99? " + (!x));
24
25          // Logical NOT '!' operator (parenthesis is optional surrounding this operator and operand)
26          System.out.println("What is the result of Not 99 > 100? " + !y);
27      }
28  }
```

Figure 3.6 – Logical and Bitwise Operator Examples

Program Output:
```
What is the result of 100 > 99 && 99 > 100? false
What is the result of 100 > 99 & 99 > 100? false
What is the result of 100 > 99 || 99 > 100? true
```

3 Tips To Master Selenium Within 30 Days
http://tinyurl.com/3-Tips-For-Selenium

Free Webinars, Videos, and Live Trainings
http://tinyurl.com/Free-QTP-UFT-Selenium

```
What is the result of 100 > 99 | 99 > 100? true
What is the result of 100 > 99 ^ 99 > 100? true
What is the result of Not 100 > 99? false
What is the result of Not 99 > 100? True
```

In this example, line five declares and initializes the variables. Both variables "x and y" are assigned boolean expressions. Variable "x" is assigned a true expression (100 > 99) while "y" is assigned a false expression (99 > 100). A && (Logical AND) operator in line eight and & (Bitwise AND) operator in line 11 compares the operands "x and y" then returns a "false" value. False is returned because one operand "x" is true while the other operand "y" is false. A similar process is performed for all examples in Figure 3.6 using different Bitwise and Logical Operators according to Figure 3.4 and Figure 3.5.

Short-Circuit Behavior Operators

Short-circuit behavior operators are || (Logical OR) and && (Logical AND) operators. Notice from Figure 3.6, || (Logical OR) and && (Logical AND) operators return the same result as | (Bitwise OR) and & (Bitwise AND) operators. However, the distinguishing characteristic relies on evaluating the operands.

If the first operand returns false then the && (Logical AND) Operator will not evaluate the second operator. Yet, the & (Bitwise AND) Operator always evaluate both operands. Likewise, the || (Logical OR) Operator will not evaluate the second operand if the first operand returns true. Contrary to the || (Logical OR) Operator, the | (Bitwise OR) Operator will always evaluate both operands.

Note: The short-circuit behavior operators do not evaluate the second operator because it knows the result regardless of the second operand.

Relational Operators

Relational Operators return a boolean value after comparing operands. Normally, all of the Relational Operators are applied to operands that are numbers. If the relationship between

Skype: rex.jones34
Twitter: @RexJonesII
Email: Rex.Jones@Test4Success.org
LinkedIn: https://www.linkedin.com/in/rexjones34

two operands is Yes, then True is returned. For example, if 34 is equal to 34, then True is returned. The following is a list of Relational Operators:

1. == (Equal To) operator
2. != (Not Equal To) operator
3. > (Greater Than) operator
4. >= (Greater Than or Equal To) operator
5. < (Less Than) operator
6. <= (Less Than or Equal To) operator

Operator	Description
==	Verifies if both operands are equal.
!=	Verifies if both operands are not equal.
>	Verifies if the left operand is greater than the right operand
>=	Verifies if the left operand is greater than or equal to the right operand
<	Verifies if the left operand is less than the right operand
<=	Verifies if the left operand is less than or equal to the right operand

Figure 3.7 – Relational Operators

The following are examples of each relational operator:

```java
1   public class Operators
2   {
3     public static void main (String[] args)
4     {
5         int x = 25, y = 50;
6
7         // = = Equal To operator
8         System.out.println("Is 25 equal to 50? " + (x == y));
9
10        // ! = Not Equal To operator
11        System.out.println("Is 25 not equal to 50? " + (x != y));
12
13        // > Greater Than operator
14        System.out.println("Is 25 greater than 50? " + (x > y));
15
16        // > = Greater Than or Equal To operator
17        System.out.println("Is 25 greater than or equal to 50? " + (x >= y));
18
19        // < Less Than operator
20        System.out.println("Is 25 less than 50? " + (x < y));
21
22        // < = Less Than or Equal To operator
23        System.out.println("Is 25 less than or equal to 50? " + (x <= y));
24    }
25  }
```

Figure 3.8 – Relational Operator Examples

Skype: rex.jones34
Twitter: @RexJonesII
Email: Rex.Jones@Test4Success.org
LinkedIn: https://www.linkedin.com/in/rexjones34

Chapter 3
Operators   (Part 1) Java 4 Selenium WebDriver

Program Output:
```
Is 25 equal to 50? false
Is 25 not equal to 50? true
Is 25 greater than 50? false
Is 25 greater than or equal to 50? false
Is 25 less than 50? true
Is 25 less than or equal to 50? True
```

In this example, line five declares and initializes the variables. Variable "x" is assigned 25 while "y" is assigned 50. An $==$ (Equal To) operator determines if both variables (x == y) equals each other on line eight. The values 25 and 50 are not equal so false is returned. A similar process is performed for all examples in Figure 3.8 using a different Relational Operator according to Figure 3.7.

Assignment Operator

An Assignment Operator (=) is positioned between a variable and value. The purpose is to assign values to variables. Therefore, the value on the right side is transferred into the variable name which is on the left side. The following is an assignment operator syntax:

Syntax
variableName = expression;

Syntax Details

Argument	Description
variableName	Name of variable that was declared
expression	Value that is assigned to the variable name
;	Semi-colon completes the initialization statement

Figure 3.9 – Assignment Operator Syntax Details

Note: The Assignment Operator can generate a chain of assignments. An assignment chain is a good way to initialize multiple variables the same value. In addition, a value is overwritten if the variable has an existing value. The following is an Assignment Operator example:

```
1   public class Operators
2   {
3       public static void main (String[] args)
4       {
5           int i, j, k;
6
7           i = j = k = 34;
8           System.out.println("The value of i is: " + i);
9           System.out.println("The value of j is: " + j);
10          System.out.println("The value of k is: " + k);
11
12          j = 38;
13          System.out.println("The value of j has been overwritten to: " + j);
14      }
15  }
```

Assignment Chain

The value **34** is assigned to variable names **i, j, and k**

The value 34 has been overwritten to **38** for variable name **j**

Figure 3.10 – Assignment Operator Example

Program Output:
```
The value of i is: 34
The value of j is: 34
The value of k is: 34
The value of j has been overwritten to: 38
```

Line five declares each variable "i, j, k" with an int data type. Line seven utilizes a chain assignment then initialize each variable the same value 34 with one statement. Line 12 overwrite variable "j" by assigning a value of 38.

Skype: rex.jones34
Twitter: @RexJonesII
Email: Rex.Jones@Test4Success.org
LinkedIn: https://www.linkedin.com/in/rexjones34

Chapter 3
Operators   (Part 1) Java 4 Selenium WebDriver

Compound Assignments

Compound Assignments (known as Shorthand Assignments) join Arithmetic and Bitwise
Operators with the Assignment Operator. The following operators are excluded from the
joining feature: increment, decrement, and one's compliment. This process shortens the
assignment statement. For example, the following two statements produce the same output:

y = y + 3;

y += 3;

Both statements assign to variable "y" the value of "y" plus three. The following is a list of
compound assignments:

1. += (Add and Assignment) operator
2. -= (Subtract and Assignment) operator
3. *= (Multiply and Assignment) operator
4. /= (Divide and Assignment) operator
5. %= (Modulus and Assignment) operator
6. &= (Bitwise And and Assignment) operator
7. |= (Bitwise OR and Assignment) operator
8. ^= (Bitwise exclusive OR (XOR) and Assignment) operator
9. <<= (Left shift and Assignment) operator
10. >>= (Right shift and Assignment) operator
11. >>>= (Unsigned right shift and Assignment) operator

Compound Assignment	Description
+=	Assigns the addition outcome
-=	Assigns the subtraction outcome
*=	Assigns the multiplication outcome
/=	Assigns the division outcome
%=	Assigns the division remainder outcome

3 Tips To Master Selenium Within 30 Days
http://tinyurl.com/3-Tips-For-Selenium

Free Webinars, Videos, and Live Trainings
http://tinyurl.com/Free-QTP-UFT-Selenium

&=	Assigns the bitwise AND outcome
|=	Assigns the bitwise OR outcome
^=	Assigns the bitwise exclusive OR (XOR) outcome
<<=	Assigns the signed left bit shift outcome
>>=	Assigns the signed right bit shift outcome
>>>=	Assigns the unsigned right bit shift outcome

Figure 3.11 – Compound Assignments

Ternary Operator

According to dictionary.com, ternary means, "consisting of or involving three." Therefore, the Ternary Operator (?) requires three operands. This operator is used to evaluate boolean expressions and determine which value is assigned to the variable. The following is the ternary operator syntax:

Syntax
variableType variableName = expression1 ? expression2 : expression3;

Syntax Details

Argument	Description
variableType	Data type of variable
variableName	Name of variable that will receive a value
expression1	Boolean expression
expression2	Value if the boolean expression is true
:	Colon separates the values of expression2 and expression3
expression3	Value if the boolean expression is false
;	Semi-colon completes the ternary operator statement

Figure 3.12 – Ternary Operator Syntax Details

Skype: rex.jones34
Twitter: @RexJonesII
Email: Rex.Jones@Test4Success.org
LinkedIn: https://www.linkedin.com/in/rexjones34

The following is a ternary operator example:

```
1  public class Operators
2  {
3     public static void main (String[] args)
4     {
5         int x, y;
6
7         x = 5;
8         System.out.println("What is the value of x? " + x);
9
10        y = (x == 5) ? 7 : 1;
11        System.out.println("x equals 5 so the boolean expression is true: Value is " + y);
12
13        y = (x == 3) ? 7 : 1;
14        System.out.println("x does not equal 3 so the boolean expression is false: Value is " + y);
15     }
16  }
```

Boolean expression = (x == 5)
y = 7 if true
y = 1 if false

Boolean expression = (x == 3)
y = 7 if true
y = 1 if false

Figure 3.13 – Ternary Operator Example

Program Output:
```
What is the value of x? 5
x equals 5 so the boolean expression is true: Value is 7
x does not equal 3 so the boolean expression is false: Value is 1
```

Line 10 displays expression1 as (x == 5) while line 13 displays expression1 as (x == 3). Both lines display expression2 as 7 and expression3 as 1. If the boolean expressions are True then variable "y" is assigned 7, otherwise "y" is assigned 1.

Operator Precedence

The operator precedence is ranking Java's operators from high to low. Rankings become important when a given expression has multiple operators. An expression is evaluated from left to right and the operator with a higher precedence receives the first evaluation. To change the precedence order, a parenthesis should be implemented to point out which expression is evaluated first. The following example shows two expressions which exclude and include a parenthesis:

```
1  public class Operators
2  {
3      public static void main (String[] args)
4      {
5          int total;
6
7          total = 2 + 3 * 4;
8          System.out.println("What is the total without a parenthesis? " + total);
9
10         total = (2 + 3) * 4;
11         System.out.println("What is the total with a parenthesis? " + total);
12     }
13 }
```

3 * 4 is evaluated before **2 + 3** because the multiplication operator (*) has a higher ranking

(2 + 3) which includes a parenthesis is evaluated before the multiplication operator (*)

Figure 3.14 – Operator Precedence Example

Program Output:
```
What is the total without a parenthesis? 14
What is the total with a parenthesis? 20
```

Typically, a Multiplication (*) Operator is evaluated before an Addition (+) Operator. The variable "total" is assigned the same values in line seven and line 10. However, the statement in line 7 do not contain parenthesis while line 10 contain parenthesis. In line 7, the Multiplication (*) Operator is evaluated first for values 3 * 4 then value 2 is added via Addition (+) Operator. Therefore, the value 14 (3 * 4 = 12 and 12 + 2 = 14) is assigned to variable "total" in line 7. In line 10, the parenthesis ranks higher than the Multiplication (*)

Skype: rex.jones34
Twitter: @RexJonesII
Email: Rex.Jones@Test4Success.org
LinkedIn: https://www.linkedin.com/in/rexjones34

Operator. As a result, values 2 + 3 is evaluated first within the parenthesis then the Multiplication (*) Operator is evaluated. Hence, the value 20 (2 + 3 = 5 and 5 * 4 = 20) is assigned to variable "total" in line 10. According to The Java ^{TM} Tutorials, the following is an operator precedence list:

Operator	Precedence
Postfix	expr++ expr--
Unary	++expr --expr +expr -expr ~ !
multiplicative	* / %
additive	+ -
shift	<< >> >>>
relational	< > <= >= instanceof
equality	== !=
bitwise AND	&
bitwise exclusive OR	^
bitwise inclusive OR		
logical AND	&&
logical OR	||
ternary	? :
assignment	= += -= *= /= %= &= ^= |= <<= >>= >>>=

Figure 3.15 – Operator Precedence

Data Type Casting

Data type casting is when the value of a data type is converted into a different data type. For instance, the value of one numeric data type "float" can be converted to another numeric data type "double." However, the value of a boolean data type can never be converted to a numeric type. There are two types of casts/conversions:

1. Implicit Casting
2. Explicit Casting

3 Tips To Master Selenium Within 30 Days
http://tinyurl.com/3-Tips-For-Selenium

Free Webinars, Videos, and Live Trainings
http://tinyurl.com/Free-QTP-UFT-Selenium

Note: The primitive data type hierarchy from high to low is double, float, long, int, short, then byte.

Implicit Casting

Implicit casting is when a conversion takes place without an instruction to the compiler to convert one data type into another data type. This type of casting only happens for a widening conversion. Widening conversions occur automatically when the value of a specific data type is converted to a higher data type. Therefore, based on the primitive data type hierarchy, an int can be converted to a float, but an error arises when trying to convert a float to an int. The following is an implicit casting example:

```
1  public class Operators
2  {
3    public static void main (String[] args)
4    {
5      int i;
6      float f;
7
8      i = 78;
9      System.out.println("The value of int 'i' is: " + i);
10
11     f = i;
12     System.out.println("The value of float 'f' is: " + f);
13   }
14 }
```

Data type **int** has a variable named **i** that is assigned to data type **float** which has a variable named **f**

Figure 3.16 - Assignment Type Conversion Example

Program Output:
```
The value of int 'i' is: 78
The value of float 'f' is: 78.0
```

Skype: rex.jones34
Twitter: @RexJonesII
Email: Rex.Jones@Test4Success.org
LinkedIn: https://www.linkedin.com/in/rexjones34

Line five declares variable "i" with an int data type while line six declares variable "f" as a float data type. Initially, line eight assigns a value of 78 to variable "i". However, a conversion happens on line 11 which converts the data type from int to float. The value "78.0" remains the same but displays differently as a float data type. Notice the value did not lose data when converting from 78 to 78.0. The following two principles are necessary for an implicit casting:

1. Both data types must be compatible
2. Destination data type (left side) must have a higher range than the source data type (right side)

The following is a list of widening conversions according to the primitive data type hierarchy:

- byte converts to short, int, long, float, or double
- short converts int, long, float, or double
- char converts to int, long, float, or double
- int converts to long, float, or double
- long converts float or double
- float converts to double

Explicit Casting

Explicit casting is when a conversion takes place with an instruction to the compiler to convert one data type into another data type. This type of casting can happen for a widening and narrowing conversion. Narrowing conversion occurs when the value of a specific data type is converted to a lower data type. Consequently, an error will not be generated when converting a float to an int. The following is an explicit casting syntax:

Syntax
(targetDataType) expression;

3 Tips To Master Selenium Within 30 Days
http://tinyurl.com/3-Tips-For-Selenium

Free Webinars, Videos, and Live Trainings
http://tinyurl.com/Free-QTP-UFT-Selenium

(Part 1) Java 4 Selenium WebDriver

Syntax Details

Argument	Description
targetDataType	Desired data type to convert the expression
expression	Value that will be converted
;	Semi-colon completes the explicit casting statement

Figure 3.17 – Explicit Casting Syntax Details

The following is an explicit casting example:

```
1  public class Operators
2  {
3      public static void main (String[] args)
4      {
5          int i = 8;
6          double d = (double) i;

8          System.out.println("What is the value of int 'i'? " + i);
9          System.out.println("What is the value of double 'd'? " + d);
10
11         float f = 12.34f;
12         short s = (short) f;
13
14         System.out.println("What is the value of float 'f'? " + f);
15         System.out.println("What is the value of short 's'? " + s);
16     }
17 }
```

Explicit Widening Conversion

Variable **i** is an **int** data type is converted to variable **d** which is a **double** data type

Narrowing Widening Conversion

Variable **f** is a **float** data type converted to variable **s** which is a **short** data type

Figure 3.18 – Explicit Casting Example

Program Output:
```
What is the value of int 'i'? 8
```

Skype: rex.jones34
Twitter: @RexJonesII
Email: Rex.Jones@Test4Success.org
LinkedIn: https://www.linkedin.com/in/rexjones34

```
What is the value of double 'd'? 8.0
What is the value of float 'f'? 12.34
What is the value of short 's'? 12
```

Line five assigns "8" to data type int, which is named "i." An explicit widening conversion ensues at line six when variable "i"—an int data type—converts to a double data type. Line 11 assigns 12.34 (a default data type of double), but converts it to a float data type 12.34f. Variable "f" holds a 12.34 value, then converts to a short data type in line 12. Notice that the value loses data on line 15, when the narrowing conversion takes place and converts a float value "12.34" to a short value of "12." The following is a list of narrowing conversions according to the primitive data type hierarchy:

- byte converts to char
- short converts to byte or char
- char converts byte or short
- int converts to byte, short, or char
- long converts to byte, short, char, or int
- float converts to byte, short, char, int, or long
- double converts byte, short, char, int, long, or float

Expressions

Operators, variables, constants, and methods (calls and returns) are components of an expression. A component joined with an operator forms an expression. It is possible to create a compound expression by combining multiple expressions. However, the data types must be compatible to construct a valid compound expression. For example, an int data type can be mixed with a long data type because both are numeric.

Through the use of type promotion rules, the mixture of data types is converted to the same data type. Values that are returned from an expression depend on the data type. Data types char, byte, and short are advanced to int. An expression is promoted to long if one of the operands is a long data type. The same goes for float data types, if one of the operands is a float then the whole expression is a float. Likewise, an expression is promoted to a double data type if one of the operands is a double. The following is an expression example with mix data types byte and float:

```
1  public class Operators
2  {
3    public static void main (String[] args)
4    {
5      byte b = 7;
6      float f = 34.56f;
7
8      float total = (b * f);
9      System.out.println("The total of byte 'b' times float 'f' (7 * 34.56) is: " + total);
10   }
11 }
```

Mix of data types byte and float (b * f) expression is promoted to float

Figure 3.19 – Expression Example

Program Output:
```
The total of byte 'b' times float 'f' (7 * 34.56) is: 241.92001
```

Line five declares and assigns a byte data type while line seven declares and assigns a float data type. On line eight, the * (Multiplication) operator multiplies both data types (byte and float) even though the types are mixed. However, the expression is promoted as a float since one of the operands is a float.

Chapter 3 gave an account for the four types of Java operators: Arithmetic, Bitwise, Logical, and Relational. The Assignment Operator and Ternary Operator were examined along with rankings of each operator. Chapter 4 will explain the two types of control structures:

branches and loops. There are two types of branches: the <u>if branch</u> and the <u>switch branch</u>. There are three types of loops: <u>for loop</u>, <u>while loop</u>, and <u>do while loop</u>.

Chapter 4
Control Structures

Control structures are the process of using logic to force the program to skip statements while looping other statements. Forcing the program to skip statements is known as branching and looping specific statements is carried out via loops.

The two types of branches are if branch and switch branch. The three types of loops are for loop, while loop, and do while loop. In addition to the branches and loops are jump statements. Jump statements allow execution to bypass unnecessary components of the program. The jump statements utilize keywords break and continue. Both keywords can be included within all branches and loops.

Chapter four will cover the following regarding control structures:

- ✓ If Branch
- ✓ Switch Branch
- ✓ For Loop
- ✓ While Loop
- ✓ Do While Loop
- ✓ Break To Exit
- ✓ Continue To Next Statement

If Branch

The if branch executes a statement when a condition is true. In other words, a specific statement is executed if a condition is met. An if branch is a greatly utilized and indispensable control structure. The following is the syntax for the if branch:

Skype: rex.jones34
Twitter: @RexJonesII
Email: Rex.Jones@Test4Success.org
LinkedIn: https://www.linkedin.com/in/rexjones34

Chapter 4
Control Structures   (Part 1) Java 4 Selenium WebDriver

Syntax
if (condition)
{
   statement(s);
}

Syntax Details

Argument	Description
if	Keyword that starts the if branch
condition	Boolean expression which results in a true or false result
{	An opening curly bracket
statement(s)	Statement that will be executed if the condition is true
;	Semi-colon completes the true statement
}	A closing curly bracket

Figure 4.1 – If Branch Syntax Details

The following example displays a message if the customer brings three extra customers to a sporting event:

Chapter 4
Control Structures   (Part 1) Java 4 Selenium WebDriver

```java
1  public class ControlStructures
2  {
3    public static void main (String[] args)
4    {
5       int extraCustomers = 4;
6
7       if (extraCustomers >= 3)
8       {
9          System.out.println("Customer receives a discount");
10      }
11   }
12 }
```

If Branch holds a boolean expression which is a condition **(extraCustomers >=3)**

Figure 4.2 – If Branch

Program Output:
```
Customer receives a discount
```

Line five assigns "4" to the variable "extraCustomers". Line seven displays keyword "if" followed by a parenthesis. Inside the parenthesis is a condition (extraCustomers >= 3) that returns true. True is returned because four is greater than three. The statement at line nine (inside the curly brackets) is executed after the true evaluation.

Note: The program would not execute the statement if the condition returned false. However, there are two variations of the if branch that can be executed when a condition is false:

1. If Else
2. If Else-If

If Else Branch
An optional else keyword extends the if branch just in case the condition returns false. Therefore, the statements following keyword "if" and the condition is executed when a

Chapter 4
Control Structures   (Part 1) Java 4 Selenium WebDriver

condition is true. Otherwise, the statement following keyword <u>else</u>, is executed when a condition is false. The following is the syntax for the if-else branch:

Syntax
if (condition)
{
   statement(s);
}
else
{
   statement(s);
}

The following example displays a message when the customer does not bring three extra customers to a sporting event:

```
 1  public class ControlStructures
 2  {
 3⊖    public static void main (String[] args)
 4      {
 5        int extraCustomers = 2;
 6
 7        if (extraCustomers >= 3)
 8        {
 9           System.out.println("Customer receives a discount");
10        }
11        else
12        {
13           System.out.println("Customer does not receive a discount");
14        }
15      }
16  }
```

> The condition **(extraCustomers >= 3)** returns **false** then executes the statement following **else** keyword

Figure 4.3 – If Else Branch

Program Output:

```
Customer does not receive a discount
```

Line five assigns "2" to the variable "extraCustomers". Line seven displays keyword "if" followed by a parenthesis. Inside the parenthesis is a condition (extraCustomers >= 3) that returns false. False is returned because two is not greater than or equal to three. Therefore, the program bypasses the statement at line nine and executes the statement at line 13.

Note: Curly brackets are optional if there is a single statement following keywords "if" and "else". However, the curly brackets are required if multiple statements exist. It is recommended to always use curly brackets to improve readability. The following is an example that does not use curly brackets:

Skype: rex.jones34
Twitter: @RexJonesII
Email: Rex.Jones@Test4Success.org
LinkedIn: https://www.linkedin.com/in/rexjones34

Chapter 4
Control Structures   (Part 1) Java 4 Selenium WebDriver

```
 1  public class ControlStructures
 2  {
 3      public static void main (String[] args)
 4      {
 5          int extraCustomers = 2;
 6
 7          if (extraCustomers >= 3)
 8              System.out.println("Customer receives a discount");
 9              System.out.println("Congratulations");
10          else
11              System.out.println("Customer does not receive a discount");
12      }
13  }
```

> Curly brackets are required to surround statements in line 8 and 9 because they are multiple statements. However, curly brackets are not required for single statement on line 11.

Figure 4.4 – No Curly Brackets

Line eight and nine are multiple statements for the if branch and require the curly brackets. Notice the red X at line 10. The red X indicates an error for the previous statements. However, an error does not exist for line 11 because it is a single statement and does not require the curly brackets.

If Else-if Branch

The first if keyword can optionally be followed by one or more if keywords. However, each subsequent if keyword must be preceded by a required else keyword. The else-if branch is only executed when the first if branch is false. All else-if branches are followed by a condition and one or more statements. The following is the syntax for the else if branch:

Syntax
```
if (condition)
{
   statement(s);
}
```

3 Tips To Master Selenium Within 30 Days
http://tinyurl.com/3-Tips-For-Selenium

Free Webinars, Videos, and Live Trainings
http://tinyurl.com/Free-QTP-UFT-Selenium

```
else if (condition)
{
   statement(s);
}
else if (condition)
{
   statement(s);
}
else
{
   statement(s);
}
```

The following example displays a message when the customer brings less than three extra customers to a sporting event:

Chapter 4
Control Structures   (Part 1) Java 4 Selenium WebDriver

```java
 1  public class ControlStructures
 2  {
 3    public static void main (String[] args)
 4    {
 5       int extraCustomers = 2;
 6
 7       if (extraCustomers >= 3)
 8       {
 9          System.out.println("Customer receives a discount");
10       }
11       else if (extraCustomers <= 3)
12       {
13          System.out.println("No Discount: Customer count less than or equal to 3");
14       }
15       else
16       {
17          System.out.println("Error: Not a valid customer count");
18       }
19    }
20  }
```

> The else if branch is executed if the first if branch is false

Figure 4.5 – Else If Branch

Program Output:

No Discount: Customer count less than or equal to 3

Line five assigns "2" to the variable "extraCustomers". Line 11 display keywords "else" and "if" followed by a parenthesis. Inside the parenthesis is a condition (extraCustomers <= 3) that returns true. True is returned because two is less than or equal to three. The second condition (line 11) is only executed after the first condition (line seven) is false.

Note: Several else-if branches can be added to the if branch:

3 Tips To Master Selenium Within 30 Days
http://tinyurl.com/3-Tips-For-Selenium

Free Webinars, Videos, and Live Trainings
http://tinyurl.com/Free-QTP-UFT-Selenium

Nested If Branch

The nested if branch consists of an if or else-if branch inside an if, else, or else-if branch. A particular outer if branch serves as a nest for the inner branch. The following is a nested if branch example:

```
1  public class ControlStructures
2  {
3     public static void main (String[] args)
4     {
5        int extraCustomers = 15;
6
7        if (extraCustomers >= 3)
8        {
9           System.out.println("Customer receives a discount");
10
11          if (extraCustomers >= 10)
12          {
13             System.out.println("25% off the price");
14          }
15          else
16          {
17             System.out.println("10% off the price");
18          }
19       }
20       else
21       {
22          System.out.println("Customer does not receive a discount");
23       }
24    }
25 }
```

The if-else branch is nested inside the if branch

Figure 4.6 – Nested If Branch

Program Output:
```
Customer receives a discount
25% off the price
```

Page | **91**

Chapter 4
Control Structures   (Part 1) Java 4 Selenium WebDriver

The nested if branch starts at line 11 and ends at line 18. A condition (extraCustomers >= 10) determines if the customer receives 10 or 25 percent off. In this case, the variable "extraCustomers" is assigned 15 at line five. Therefore, the condition at line 11 evaluates to true and executes the first statement "25% off the price." The second statement would execute if the variable "extraCustomers" is less than 10.

Switch Branch

The switch branch evaluates a single variable then executes a statement according to the variable's value. Primitive data types byte, short, char, and int can be evaluated along with String. The switch and if branches are similar in functionality. There are situations where either branch is suitable. However, the switch branch is most efficient when dealing with a specific number of values, such as days of the week. Otherwise, it is best to implement an if branch when handling an infinite number of values. The following is the syntax for the switch branch:

Syntax
```
switch (variableName)
{
case constant1:
   statement(s);
   break;
case constant2:
   statement(s);
   break;
case constant3:
   statement(s);
   break;
.

.
```

.

```
default:
  statement;

}
```

Syntax Details

Argument	Description
switch	Checks the variable's value
variableName	Name of the variable
{	An opening curly bracket
case constant1, 2, 3 …	Contains a possible match for the variable's value
statement(s)	Statement to be executed if the variable's value match a given case
;	Semi-colon completes a statement
break	An optional keyword that exits out of the switch branch
;	Semi-colon completes the break
default	An optional keyword that will execute if the variable's value does not match a case
statement	Default statement to be executed if the variable's value does not match a case
}	A closing curly bracket

Figure 4.7 – Switch Branch Syntax Details

Skype: rex.jones34
Twitter: @RexJonesII
Email: Rex.Jones@Test4Success.org
LinkedIn: https://www.linkedin.com/in/rexjones34

The following is a switch branch example:

```
1  public class ControlStructures
2  {
3    public static void main (String[] args)
4    {
5      int day = 6;
6
7      switch (day)
8      {
9      case 1:
10        System.out.println("Sunday is the 1st day of the week");
11        break;
12      case 2:
13        System.out.println("Monday is the 2nd day of the week");
14        break;
15      case 3:
16        System.out.println("Tuesday is the 3rd day of the week");
17        break;
18      case 4:
19        System.out.println("Wednesday is the 4th day of the week");
20        break;
21      case 5:
22        System.out.println("Thursday is the 5th day of the week");
23        break;
24      case 6:
25        System.out.println("Friday is the 6th day of the week");
26        break;
27      case 7:
28        System.out.println("Saturday is the 7th day of the week");
29        break;
30      default:
31        System.out.println("Not valid: There are only 7 days in a week");
32      }
33    }
34  }
```

Switch branch for 7 days of the week

Figure 4.8 – Switch Branch Example

Program Output:
Friday is the 6th day of the week

3 Tips To Master Selenium Within 30 Days
http://tinyurl.com/3-Tips-For-Selenium

Free Webinars, Videos, and Live Trainings
http://tinyurl.com/Free-QTP-UFT-Selenium

Line five assigns the variable "day" the value of "6." Then the keyword "switch" starts the branch at line seven by checking the variable's value. Keyword "case" at line 24 matches the variable's value "6", then executes the statement at line 25. The keyword "break" at line 26 is necessary to prevent case 7 (line 27) and default (line 30) from executing.

Note: All statements following a match will execute due to switch branches executing sequentially utilizing a top-down approach. Therefore, the keyword "break" must be used to jump out of the switch branch after a match is found.

Nested Switch Branch

The nested switch branch consists of a switch branch inside another switch branch. In addition, an if branch can be nested inside of a switch branch. The outer switch branch serves as a nest for the inner branch. Values are unique to their respective outer and inner branch. For instance, a constant can contain the same value in multiple switch branches. The following is a switch branch example:

Chapter 4
Control Structures
(Part 1) Java 4 Selenium WebDriver

```
1  public class ControlStructures
2  {
3    public static void main (String[] args)
4    {
5      int day = 2, numHours = 4;
6
7      switch (day)
8      {
9      case 1:
10         System.out.println("Sunday is the 1st day of the week");
11         break;
12      case 2:
13         System.out.println("Monday is the 2nd day of the week");
14      switch (numHours)
15      {
16      case 4:
17         System.out.println("Plan to work 4 hours (half a day) due to an appointment");
18         break;
19      case 8:
20         System.out.println("Plan to work 8 hours today");
21         break;
22      default:
23         System.out.println("Not sure how many hours I will work today");
24         break;
25      }
26         break;
27      case 3:
28         System.out.println("Tuesday is the 3rd day of the week");
29         break;
30      case 4:
31         System.out.println("Wednesday is the 4th day of the week");
32         break;
```

Nested Switch Branch

The switch branch is nested inside case **2**. The same constant value **4** can be used in the outer and inner switch branch

Figure 4.9 – Nested Switch Branch

Program Output:

```
Monday is the 2nd day of the week
Plan to work 4 hours (half a day) due to an appointment
```

3 Tips To Master Selenium Within 30 Days
http://tinyurl.com/3-Tips-For-Selenium

Free Webinars, Videos, and Live Trainings
http://tinyurl.com/Free-QTP-UFT-Selenium

Chapter 4
Control Structures   (Part 1) Java 4 Selenium WebDriver

Line five assigns the variable "numHours" the value of "4." Then the keyword "switch"
starts the nested switch branch at line 14 by checking the variable's value. The nested switch
branch encompasses two cases and one default. One of the cases at line 16 hold the same
constant, "4", as an outer case at line 30.

For Loop

The for loop executes a block of code for a certain number of iterations. In other words, a
statement is executed as long as a condition is met. One of the for loop benefits is to allow
statements to be executed without writing code repeatedly. The following is the for loop
syntax:

Syntax
for (initialization; condition; iteration)
{
   statement(s)
}

Syntax Details

Argument	Description
for	Keyword that starts the for loop
initialization	Assignment that sets the loop control initial value
;	Semi-colon completes the initialization
condition	A boolean expression that determines if the loop will or will not repeat
;	Semi-colon completes the condition
iteration	Indicates how the loop control variable will change after each variation
{	An opening curly bracket
statement(s)	Statement(s) that will execute after the condition is met
;	Semi-colon completes the statement

}	A closing curly bracket

Figure 4.10 – For Loop Syntax Details

The initialization component declares a data type and assigns an initial value via loop control variable. Usually, the loop control variable is a single character variable name (e.g., i) that controls the entire loop. The condition is a boolean expression that specifies a maximum value for the loop control variable. All for loops continue executing while the condition is true. Execution begins on the statement immediately following the for loop when the condition becomes false. Most automation engineers use an increment (++) or decrement (--) operator as the iteration expression. The increment operator increases the loop control variable by one, while the decrement operator decreases the value by one. An executable statement is placed between the optional curly brackets. Although, the curly brackets are optional, it is recommended to use the brackets to improve readability. The following is a for loop example:

```
1  public class ControlStructures
2  {
3      public static void main (String[] args)
4      {
5          for (int i = 0; i < 5; i++ )
6          {
7              System.out.println("The loop control variable value is " + i);
8          }
9      }
10 }
```

For Loop

(Initialization) int i = 0;
(Condition) i < 5;
(Iteration) i++

Figure 4.11 – For Loop Example

Program Output:
```
The loop control variable value is 0
The loop control variable value is 1
```

3 Tips To Master Selenium Within 30 Days
http://tinyurl.com/3-Tips-For-Selenium

Free Webinars, Videos, and Live Trainings
http://tinyurl.com/Free-QTP-UFT-Selenium

```
The loop control variable value is 2
The loop control variable value is 3
The loop control variable value is 4
```

Line five starts the for loop with keyword "for" followed by arguments initialization, condition, and iteration. Initialization (int i = 0;) assigns zero as the starting value. Condition (i < 5) sets five as the stopping point for the loop control variable. Increment (i++) increases the loop control variable by one. The statement prints the loop control variable via line seven.

It is important to use harmonious values in the for loop. The values can lead to an infinite loop if they are not created in agreement. An infinite loop is a loop that never stops. For example, the following for loop will repeat indefinitely because of the initial value, maximum value, and iteration expression:

for (int i = 3; i > 1; i++)

The initial value "3" starts at a greater value than the maximum value of "1," while the iterator "++" increases after each loop. To correct this infinite loop, the initialization value "3" must decrease to less than the conditional value "1"; the conditional value "1" must increase to more than the initialization "3"; or the iterator must change from increasing "++" to decreasing "--" after each loop.

Note: Routinely, a condition using a greater than operator (>) implements a decrement operator (--), while a condition using a less than operator (<) implements an increment operator (++).

Nested For Loop

The nested for loop consist of a for loop inside another for loop. An outer for loop serves as a nest for the inner loop. Statements within the inner loop can utilize the loop control variables from the outer loop. As a result, it is best to use different loop control variables for each loop. The following is a nested for loop example:

Chapter 4
Control Structures   (Part 1) Java 4 Selenium WebDriver

```
1   public class ControlStructures
2   {
3     public static void main (String[] args)
4     {
5       for (int x = 0; x < 3; x++ )
6       {
7         System.out.println("Outer Loop value is " + x);
8         for (int y = 0; y < 3; y++ )
9         {
10          System.out.println("   Inner Loop value is " + y);
11        }
12      }
13    }
14  }
```

Inner For Loop

(Initialization) **int y = 0;**
(Condition) **y < 3;**
(Iteration) **y++**

Figure 4.12 – Nested For Loop

Program Output:
```
Outer Loop value is 0
   Inner Loop value is 0
   Inner Loop value is 1
   Inner Loop value is 2
Outer Loop value is 1
   Inner Loop value is 0
   Inner Loop value is 1
   Inner Loop value is 2
Outer Loop value is 2
   Inner Loop value is 0
   Inner Loop value is 1
   Inner Loop value is 2
```

Line eight starts the nested for loop with keyword "for" followed by arguments initialization, condition, and iteration. Initialization (int y = 0;) assigns zero as the starting value. Condition (y < 3) sets three as the stopping point for the loop control variable. Increment (y++) increases the loop control variable by one. The statement prints the loop control variable via line 10.

3 Tips To Master Selenium Within 30 Days
http://tinyurl.com/3-Tips-For-Selenium

Free Webinars, Videos, and Live Trainings
http://tinyurl.com/Free-QTP-UFT-Selenium

While Loop

The while loop repeats a statement while a condition is true. Conditions are boolean expressions that is checked prior to executing the statement. In addition, the variable name is initialized before the loop and evaluated as part of the condition. When executing the statement, the while loop continues until the condition becomes false. The following is the syntax of a while loop.

Syntax
while (condition)
{
  statement(s);
}

Syntax Details

Argument	Description
while	Keyword that starts the loop
condition	A boolean expression that determines if the loop will or will not repeat
{	An opening curly bracket
statement(s)	Statement(s) that will execute after the condition is met
;	Semi-colon that completes the statement
}	A closing curly bracket

Figure 4.13 – While Loop Syntax Details

The following is a while loop example:

Skype: rex.jones34
Twitter: @RexJonesII
Email: Rex.Jones@Test4Success.org
LinkedIn: https://www.linkedin.com/in/rexjones34

Chapter 4
Control Structures   (Part 1) Java 4 Selenium WebDriver

```
1   public class ControlStructures
2   {
3°     public static void main (String[] args)
4      {
5        int i = 0;
6
7        while (i < 5)
8        {
9           System.out.println("The variables value is " + i);
10          i++;
11       }
12     }
13  }
```

> Variable name i initialized to zero (0) and while loop starts with keyword **while**. The loop executes while condition (**i < 5**) remains true

Figure 4.14 – While Loop Example

Program Output:
```
The variables value is 0
The variables value is 1
The variables value is 2
The variables value is 3
The variables value is 4
```

Line five initializes the variable "i" to zero "0". The variable will be evaluated at line seven as part of the condition (i < 5) after keyword "while". A value for the variable "i" is repeatedly printed via line nine while the condition is true. Notice the increment operator at line 10. It is important to know that the while loop never stops if the increment operator is not added. Therefore, the loop would continue indefinitely, generating an infinite loop. In addition, the while loop becomes indefinite if the initialization and conditional variable values are not set in agreement.

Do While Loop

The do while loop evaluates a condition at the bottom of the loop. Therefore, the loop will execute the statement within the loop then evaluate the condition. As a result, the do while loop always executes a statement for at least one iteration and continues as long as the condition is true. The following is the syntax for a do while loop:

Syntax
```
do
{
   statement(s);
}
while (condition);
```

Syntax Details

Argument	Description
do	Keyword that starts the loop
{	An opening curly bracket
statement(s)	Statement(s) that will execute at least once
;	Semi-colon that completes the statement
}	A closing curly bracket
while	Keyword that determines if the loop's condition will repeat
condition	A boolean expression that determines if the loop will or will not repeat
;	Semi-colon that completes the condition

Figure 4.15 – Do While Loop Syntax Details

The following is a do while loop example:

Chapter 4
Control Structures   (Part 1) Java 4 Selenium WebDriver

```
1  public class ControlStructures
2  {
3      public static void main (String[] args)
4      {
5          int i = 0;
6
7          do
8          {
9              System.out.println("The variables value is " + i);
10             i++;
11         }
12         while (i < 5);
13     }
14 }
```

> Variable name i initialized to zero (0) and do while loop starts with keyword **do**. The loop executes while condition **(i < 5)** remains true

Figure 4.16 – Do While Loop Example

Program Output:
```
The variables value is 0
The variables value is 1
The variables value is 2
The variables value is 3
The variables value is 4
```

Line five initializes the variable "i" to zero "0". The keyword "do" starts the do while loop followed by two statements surrounded by curly brackets. A value for the variable "i" is repeatedly printed via line nine while the condition (i < 5) is true. Coincidentally, the condition is evaluated after the statement at line 12. Like the while loop, an infinite loop would have occurred if the increment operator (++) was not added at line 10. Also, the initialization and conditional values can create an infinite loop if not set correctly. In this example, the statements were repeated multiple iterations because the condition started with a true result. The following shows what happens when the condition starts with a false result:

3 Tips To Master Selenium Within 30 Days
http://tinyurl.com/3-Tips-For-Selenium

Free Webinars, Videos, and Live Trainings
http://tinyurl.com/Free-QTP-UFT-Selenium

Chapter 4
Control Structures   (Part 1) Java 4 Selenium WebDriver

```
1  public class ControlStructures
2  {
3      public static void main (String[] args)
4      {
5          int i = 0;
6
7          do
8          {
9              System.out.println("The variables value is " + i);
10             i++;
11         }
12         while (i > 5);
13     }
14 }
```

Variable name **i** initialized to zero (0) and do while loop starts with keyword **do**. The loop executes while condition **(i > 5)** remains true. This loop executes one time although the condition is false

Figure 4.17 – Do While Loop Example (Start With False Condition)

Program Output:
```
The variables value is 0
```

Line five initializes the variable "i" to zero "0". Therefore, the condition (i > 5) at line 12 is false due to zero being less than five. The do while loop executed the statement because statements are executed first, then the condition is evaluated.

Note: The loops (for, while, and do while) are similar in functionality. A rule of thumb to use when deciding which loop to implement is:

- Implement a for loop when executing a specific number of iterations
- Implement a while loop when the loop will repeat an uncertain number of iterations
- Implement a do while loop when a loop needs to be executed at least one iteration

Break To Exit

The "break" keyword is optional and used to force an exit from a branch or loop. If a break occurs within a nested branch or loop then the innermost branch or loop discontinues. However, execution resumes at the statement immediately following the current branch or loop. The following is a break keyword example using statements from Figure 4.8 (Switch Branch).

```java
1  public class ControlStructures
2  {
3      public static void main (String[] args)
4      {
5          int day = 6;
6
7          switch (day)
8          {
9          case 1:
10             System.out.println("Sunday is the 1st day of the week");
11             break;
12         case 2:
13             System.out.println("Monday is the 2nd day of the week");
14             break;
15         case 3:
16             System.out.println("Tuesday is the 3rd day of the week");
17             break;
18         case 4:
19             System.out.println("Wednesday is the 4th day of the week");
20             break;
21         case 5:
22             System.out.println("Thursday is the 5th day of the week");
23             break;
24         case 6:
25             System.out.println("Friday is the 6th day of the week");
26             break;
27         case 7:
28             System.out.println("Saturday is the 7th day of the week");
29             break;
30         default:
31             System.out.println("Not valid: There are only 7 days in a week");
32         }
33     }
34 }
```

The **break** keyword is used to exit each case if a match is located for that specific case

Figure 4.18 – Break Keyword Example

3 Tips To Master Selenium Within 30 Days
http://tinyurl.com/3-Tips-For-Selenium

Free Webinars, Videos, and Live Trainings
http://tinyurl.com/Free-QTP-UFT-Selenium

In this example, the "break" keyword is used to exit a case if a match is located. A match happens for case six at line 24. The break keyword prevents case seven (line 27) and the default (line 30) from executing.

Note: More than one break keyword can appear in a branch or loop. There is a break keyword after every case.

Continue To Next Statement

The "continue" keyword forces the current loop iteration to stop and immediately execute the next loop iteration. As a result, the condition and statement between both intervals are skipped. The following is an example using the "continue" keyword to skip all odd numbers:

```java
1  public class ControlStructures
2  {
3      public static void main (String[] args)
4      {
5          for (int x = 2; x <= 10; x++ )
6          {
7              if (x % 2 != 0) continue;
8              System.out.println("Even numbers " + x);
9          }
10     }
11 }
```

The **continue** keyword is used to skip all odd numbers and print all even numbers

Figure 4.19 – Continue Keyword

Program Output:
```
Even numbers 2
Even numbers 4
Even numbers 6
Even numbers 8
Even numbers 10
```

Skype: rex.jones34
Twitter: @RexJonesII
Email: Rex.Jones@Test4Success.org
LinkedIn: https://www.linkedin.com/in/rexjones34

Chapter 4
Control Structures   (Part 1) Java 4 Selenium WebDriver

Line seven implements the "continue" keyword to bypass all odd numbers. Therefore, the condition and statements are skipped when the loop control variable "i" equals one, three, five, seven, and nine.

Conclusion

The purpose of "Part 1 – Java 4 Selenium WebDriver" was to provide a good foundational knowledge of Java. An understanding of Java facilitates the process of testing an Application Under Testing (AUT) via Selenium. The key to verifying data within an AUT, is knowing how to access and manipulate data. Data is represented by variables, which can be text or numbers. All variables must have a data type to indicate the range and behavior. The data type is significant when dealing with operators because certain functions are performed according to the data type. In addition, some of the operators are contributors to forming control structures. The following items are take–away topics from the book:

Variables: A location that holds data

Data Types: Refer to a variable's type

Operators: A symbol that performs mathematical or logical operations

Control Structures: Refers to the process of using logic to force the program to skip or loop statements

The second book is titled "(Part 2) Java 4 Selenium WebDriver". It takes a closer look at Classes, Objects, and Methods while examining Object-Oriented Programming (OOP), which consist of Inheritance, Encapsulation, and Polymorphism. In addition, the book explores Packages, Interfaces, Exception Handling, and how to utilize Input/Output.

Skype: rex.jones34
Twitter: @RexJonesII
Email: Rex.Jones@Test4Success.org
LinkedIn: https://www.linkedin.com/in/rexjones34

Resources

1. Beginning Java® Programming
   The Object-Oriented Approach
   Bart Baesens, Aimée Backiel, Seppe vanden Broucke

2. Java A Beginner's Guide Sixth Edition
   Create, Compile, and Run Java Programs Today
   Herbert Schildt

3. Webopedia
   http://www.webopedia.com/TERM/A/ASCII.html

4. Dictionary.Reference.com
   http://dictionary.reference.com/browse/ternary?s=t

5. ORACLE Java Documentation
   The Java ™ Tutorials
   https://docs.oracle.com/javase/tutorial/java/nutsandbolts/operators.html

3 Tips To Master Selenium Within 30 Days
http://tinyurl.com/3-Tips-For-Selenium

Free Webinars, Videos, and Live Trainings
http://tinyurl.com/Free-QTP-UFT-Selenium

Download PDF Version

The PDF Version of this book is available to you at the following link.

http://tinyurl.com/Part-1-Java-4-Selenium

If the book was helpful, can you leave a favorable review?

http://tinyurl.com/Review-Part-1-Java-4-Selenium

Thanks in advance,

Rex Allen Jones II

Skype: rex.jones34
Twitter: @RexJonesII
Email: Rex.Jones@Test4Success.org
LinkedIn: https://www.linkedin.com/in/rexjones34

Books by Rex Jones II

www.tinyurl.com/Rex-Allen-Jones-books

1. **Free Book** Absolute Beginner
   (Part 1) You Must Learn VBScript for QTP/UFT
   Don't Ignore The Language For Functional Automation Testing

2. (Part 2) You Must Learn VBScript for QTP/UFT
   Don't Ignore The Language For Functional Automation Testing

3. **Free Book** Absolute Beginner
   (Part 1) Java 4 Selenium WebDriver
   Come Learn How To Program For Automation Testing

4. (Part 2) Java 4 Selenium WebDriver
   Come Learn How To Program For Automation Testing

5. **Free Book** Absolute Beginner
   (Part 1) Selenium WebDriver for Functional Automation Testing
   Your Beginners Guide

6. Getting Started With TestNG
   A Java Test Framework

3 Tips To Master Selenium Within 30 Days
http://tinyurl.com/3-Tips-For-Selenium

Free Webinars, Videos, and Live Trainings
http://tinyurl.com/Free-QTP-UFT-Selenium

Books by Rex Jones II   (Part 1) Java 4 Selenium WebDriver

Skype: rex.jones34
Twitter: @RexJonesII
Email: Rex.Jones@Test4Success.org
LinkedIn: https://www.linkedin.com/in/rexjones34

Sign Up To Receive

1. 3 Tips To Master Selenium Within 30 Days
   http://tinyurl.com/3-Tips-For-Selenium

2. 3 Tips To Master QTP/UFT Within 30 Days
   http://tinyurl.com/3-Tips-For-QTP-UFT

3. Free Webinars, Videos, and Live Trainings
   http://tinyurl.com/Free-QTP-UFT-Selenium